ALEXANDER A. LAWRENCE

A versatile Georgian whose presence has graced the bench, whose writing has enhanced the state's literature, and whose humor has inspired merriment in his fellow man.

TONGUE IN CHEEK

By

Alexander A. Lawrence

ATLANTA
CHEROKEE PUBLISHING COMPANY
1979

Library of Congress Catalog Card Number: 79-54272
International Standard Booksellers Number: 0-87797-047-5

Copies of *Tongue in Cheek* may be obtained through leading booksellers everywhere or by ordering direct from Cherokee Publishing Company's sales office: Post Office Box 1081, Covington, Georgia 30209, USA. Send $7.95 plus 59 cents postage. Georgia residents add 3% state sales tax and, where applicable, 1% local option tax.

PRINTED IN THE UNITED STATES OF AMERICA

Contents

The Author

Alexander A. Lawrence is a lifelong resident of Savannah who has achieved distinction as lawyer, jurist, author, historian, and civic leader.

He was born on 28 December 1906, son of Alexander A. and Isabel Ashby (Paine) Lawrence, who were representatives of families long prominently identified with Marietta, Georgia, and Charleston, South Carolina, respectively. He and his wife, the former Margaret Adams of Savannah, are the parents of Alexander A. Lawrence, Jr. and of the late Margaret Lawrence Binder.

Alex Lawrence was graduated from Woodberry Forest Preparatory School (1925) and the University of Georgia, *magna cum laude* and Phi Beta Kappa (1929). For nearly fifty years he has been a member of the bar, and since 1968 he has served as judge of the United States District Court for the Southern District of Georgia.

In the course of a long and useful career he has been president of the Savannah Rotary Club, the Savannah Chamber of Commerce, the Savannah Benevolent Association, and the Georgia Historical Society. He has been chairman of the United Community Appeal and governor of the Georgia Society of Colonial Wars. He is an Episcopalian and a Democrat.

A gifted story-teller, an eloquent writer, and a thorough scholar, Judge Lawrence's interest in history and biography has resulted in such notable volumes of Georgiana as *James Moore Wayne: Southern Unionist* (1943), *Storm Over Savannah* (1951; revised editions 1969 and 1979), *James Johnston, Georgia's First Printer* (1956), *A Present For Mr. Lincoln. The Story of Savannah From Secession to Sherman* (1961), and *Johnny Leber and the Confederate Major* (1963).

Judge Lawrence's erudition and dry humor have made him a sought-after speaker on both serious and light subjects. *Tongue In*

Cheek is a collection of some of his talks, brief remarks, and judicial opinions in the latter category. Through the pages of this volume the reader meets him at his most engaging: humorous, ironic, and deft.

William B. Williford

(A few days after this book went to press, the distinguished career of Judge Alexander A. Lawrence was ended by his unexpected death on 20 August 1979 at the age of 72. He was buried in Bonaventure Cemetery at Savannah.)

Foreword

The selections included in this volume were chosen from a collection of speeches made over a period of many years. Their facetious, light-hearted tone is a total departure from my serious historical books and articles and puts them in the broad category of what may be called humor. That really indefinable term has been aptly described as a happy compound of pathos and playfulness.

In the sense of amusement and pleasure, humor is generally defined as an action, a situation, or an expression of ideas appealing to a sense of the ludicrous or the absurdly incongruous. Wit as such is ephemeral and has been said to be less purely intellectual than humor, which has a sympathetic quality sometimes allied to pathos or the comical. "True humor . . . is not contempt," said Carlyle, "its essence is love; it issues not in laughter but in still smiles . . ."

With the exception of Stephen B. Leacock, an outstanding 20th century humorist as well as a student of the nature and technique of humor, it is unlikely that the noted humorists of the past century and half ever gave a thought to theory or technique. Like Belloc's Water Beetle, they glided "on the water's face / with ease, celerity, and grace. / But if he stopped to try and think / of how he did it, he would sink."

A distinguishable quality of English "humour" has long been understatement or meiosis. In the mid-1800s punning was the vogue but in the end a surfeited public put an end to it. I probably laid the ghost to rest in my account of the founding and early history of Georgia and in the play on words there and in one or two other selections.

Vogues in this country, both national and regional, have changed often over the years. Long ago we cut loose from the classic conceptions and definitions. I do not really know what passes for humor today. It appears to be a mongrel of disillusionment and frustration; "comedy" serials on TV with punch-lines, "one-liners", and what not.

My own idea of the humorous has been that which entertains and amuses an audience. Laughter was my object, the more the merrier. But what produces it had to be tailored to the subject and the occasion.

Whether readers will agree in classifying the selections chosen as humorous or as merely droll (or even mirthless), they provided me an occasional escape from the grind of a demanding profession.

ALEXANDER A. LAWRENCE
Savannah, Georgia
July 10, 1979

TONGUE
IN
CHEEK

Part I

A Medley of This and That

The After-Dinner Scotch

(St. Andrews Society, 225th Anniversary Banquet, Savannah, December 2, 1975.)

I am flattered by the invitation to speak on the occasion of this auspicious anniversary in the history of your Ancient and Honorable Society. Quite possibly I have in the past decade addressed societies as honorable as this one. In fact, I am sure I have, but certainly I have never spoken before a society as ancient.

I recall speaking once at a centennial banquet. Afterward, a member informed me that he thought the society would be celebrating its bicentennial before I got through. Your Speakers' Committee took care of that problem tonight. After three or four hours of indulgence by this distinguished audience in drink, song, food and mirth, you have magnanimously allotted fifteen minutes to two speakers who have waited 225 years for this event. A fine way to treat an eminent servant of the Almighty like Dr. Cleland and a federal judge who behaves like he's Almighty God!

Nonetheless, I shall respect the fifteen-minute sudden-death rule as much as I resent it as a gross invasion of a lawyer's First Amendment right to talk as long as he pleases about nothing. I leave it to Dr. Cleland to say whether the restriction on the speakers' time violates the Ten Commandments – including all the recent amendments thereto.

But I forgive and pardon the Speakers' Committee. It looks like I have to run everything except the churches, and now is a good time to get into that business. And so I bestow on the committeemen the ignominy of a Church of England benediction. And, after all, due allowance must be made for the fact that you Scotch are a special breed. When the Lord was creating our earthly sphere (it was the fourth day of Creation). He finished what we know as Scotland. The Creator had worked overtime on that particular part of the earth and sat down to rest and admire his masterpiece. And no wonder! For He had created an enchanting land – a land of

Mist-capped mountains, heathered hills,
Wooded glens and laughing rills;
Gentle rivers, roaring streams,
Blue-eyed lakes where dance sunbeams;
Wych-elms shading bonny dale,
Blue bells carpeting the vale –
Land of crag and loch and firth,
Land where heaven came to earth.

I hasten to explain that the rhymed lines you just heard are from an unknown Scotch bard – McLawrence of Lower Loch Ness.

Well, the Lord couldn't help bragging about His handiwork to one of His archangels. The archangel agreed. But he asked the Creator whether it was fair to favor one wee bit of the earth so much. The Lord thought a moment and replied, "Just wait 'till you see the kind of people I'm going to put down there."

Well, whatever mistakes He may have made in populating Scotland, the Creator at least ended up by putting some mighty fine Scots in Savannah. During the past two hundred and twenty-five years, members of your Society have furnished notable leadership in the commercial, industrial and shipping affairs of this community as well as to its cultural, political and military history.

However, the unique and surprising feature of your 225-year existence is the fact that a society of Scotchmen could survive for so long in outward harmony and fellowship without breaking up into dissenting or splinter organizations.

Someone once said that nobody's smarter than one Chinaman and nobody dumber than two Chinamen. The way I see it is that no one is cannier than one Scotchman and nobody more cantankerous than two Scotchmen. There must be a strong common bond that has held this society together for so long. I think I know what it is. I've attended your banquets (as well as those of other Savannah tippling societies) for so many years that I can almost say:

I've drunk your health in company,
I've drunk your health alone,
I've drunk your health so many times,
I've damned near ruined my own.

Instead of "A' the Bonnie Lassies" I feel like responding to the toast:

Here's to the Scotch, the Irish and Dutch
They think too little and they drink too much.

Actually, the full text of the toast is "A' the Bonnie Lassies that Whirl Amang the Heather". It does not mention the Bonny Lads. I am sure, however, they were out in the heather flushing the lassies. It's typical of them to take the girls out on the heath instead of to a dance hall or to the movies.

Tonight, you omitted that very eloquent toast of Sir Walter Scott: "I give you every river, every loch, every hill from Tweed to John O'Groat's House." Now, if that isn't genuine Scotch liberality! Sir Walter didn't own one single thing he was giving away. And he was even trying to give away poor John O'Groat's cottage.

"So much of what is great in Scotland has sprung from the closeness of the family ties." Great, too, is the sentimental attachment of Scotchmen, wherever they may live, to the land of their fathers. All year my Scotch friends speak understandable Geechee. But when St. Andrews' birthday comes around they affect a tongue-point trill and go around talking about "bra' bricht moonlicht nichts", "wee drappies", "deochs and douris" and "braes". And the way some of you transplanted Scotch dress up on these occasions – your tartans, plaids, bonnets and kilts! Burns' line comes to mind. "Oh wad some power the giftie gie to see oursels as others see us!"

But lest we who live in this part of the country forget why we speak Geechee instead of Spanish, let us gratefully remember the kilted Scotchmen who defended St. Simons Island in 1742. Let me give you the true and inside history of Bloody Marsh. On a hot July day the invading Spanish forces were marching on their way to attack Fort Frederica. Their commander was a handsome, mustachioed Spaniard named Don Manuel de Montiano. As Spaniards sometimes do, he had an eye for the senoritas. General Montiano asked his guide who those girls were up ahead of them who had come out to welcome the Spanish to Georgia. His St. Simons guide spoke English about like you Scotch do. He say, "Gen'ul Lissmo, dem ain' 'oomen, dey mon. Dem skirt foo' yuh. Dey kilt. What you t'ink underneat' . . . ."

Don Montiano had heard enough. He suddenly lost all interest in the Golden Isles of Georgia. He gathered his troops around him and announced: "The reign of Spain is over on this coastal plain." The soldiers repeated after him, "The reign of Spain is over on this plain." "The reign of Spain is over . . ." "By George, you've got it!" said Montiano just before he and his men boarded their galleons and sailed back to Cuba.

You Scotch-Americans are a nostalgic lot when it comes to the mother country. Tears run down your Rosemont tunics because the English beat "Bonny Prince Charlie" at Culloden and you cry in your cups over the sad fate that befell Mary Queen of Scots. It is easily explained. Queen Elizabeth I just didn't believe in the proverb that two heads are better than one.

But just when you reach the climax of melancholy your faces suddenly light up. Your eyes stop watering and your mouth starts to water. The ceremonial moment of the bringing in of the haggis has arrived. The origin of haggis is well known, at least to me. When your Highland ancestors got hungry (which was normal in their life-style) they would come roaring down out of the Highlands to steal sheep on the English side of the border. Then they would go back and make haggis. We find the recipe for the dish in *Macbeth*: "Eye of newt and toe of frog/ wool of bat, and tongue of dog."

After your Highland ancestors fed a few weeks on their national dish, they would build up enough strength to go back south of the border and steal some more sheep from my English forbears. In once-Merrie England the Lawrences used to follow the hounds. But things got turned around. The hounds suddenly started following the Lawrences. And so they settled in America, and damned if the hounds aren't still following me over here.

All I'm going to get out of my appearance here tonight is two Robert Burns cigars and my own haggis. What I want is my ancestral flocks. Bring back, bring back, oh, bring back our schepies to me.

These Scotch songs! You sing them with a gusto equalled only by discord. "O' ye'll tak' the high road and I'll tak' the low road" and race you to Caledonia.

"Tho' I'm far awa' frae Scotland, and the scenes I lo'e sae weel, There's a beat for the auld country that in every pulse I feel."

Well, all I can say about your nostalgia is that if Judge Lawrence ordered one single member of this society deported to the bonny braes of his ancestral home, all hell would break loose in Savannah, Georgia.

I close these remarks, for my time is up, in no spirit of jest or levity but on a note of seriousness and sincerity. The historian Edward Gibbon in dealing with the moral disintegration of the ancient city-states of the Mediterranean wrote in language poignantly relevant to America today:

> *In the end more than they wanted freedom, they wanted a comfortable life [and] security . . . When [they] finally wanted not to give to society but for society to give to them, when the freedom they wished for most was freedom from responsibility, then [they] ceased to be free.*

Mr. President, no historian can ever say that of the Scotch. In the sounding phrase of Thomas B. Macaulay: "In perseverance, in self-command, in forethought, in all the virtues which conduce to success in life, the Scots have never been surpassed."

It Is My Privilege To Present . . .

(Sixty-Seventh Annual Session of the Georgia Bar Association, Savannah, June 2, 1950. Introduction of Sen. Leverett Saltonstall of Mass.)

TOASTMASTER: It now becomes my pleasure to introduce the speaker of this occasion. This is a banner night, indeed. This is a precedent-making occasion. It was just eighty-six years ago that William T. Sherman visited our city. As Henry W. Grady said in a very notable address delivered at Boston, where our speaker lives, Sherman was a fine general, though perhaps a little careless with fire. It is a most encouraging sign, I think, for national unity that less than five score years after General Sherman was here we are able to invite the senior senator from the great Commonwealth of Masachusetts to address a Georgia audience.

It may puzzle you somewhat as to why a Republican senator from New England should be invited here. I hasten to disabuse your minds of any erroneous impressions you may have as to the political significance of that fact. This is an election year in Georgia. Politicians are as thick at this convention "as the autumnal leaves that strow the brooks in Vallombrosa," as the learned federal judge said this morning. We were anxious to get this convention as far away as possible from politics. We thought the surest way to do it was to invite here tonight a Republican United States senator from Massachusetts. In fact, we knew of no better way to eliminate any and all idea of practical politics than to bring to Savannah some one high up in the Republican Party.

Senator Saltonstall, you have a remarkable audience here tonight. When you said, as you did in a speech a few years ago, that "we want our country to be governed from the bottom up and not from the top down," that "the government under which the States rose to greatness is government that begins at home," I venture to say that 100 per cent of this audience agrees with you. But I warn you that this is a unique state and a strange people. I must tell you, Senator Saltonstall, that you have more friends and fewer supporters in this audience than any man who ever spoke here.

But do not, however, feel entirely lonely in these Deep South surroundings – Savannah has at least one connection with your party. It was here in this city that the first presidential candidate of the Republican Party was born. His name was John C. Fremont and he first saw the light of day on Broughton Street in the year 1813. The fact that Fremont was born out of wedlock and his subsequent affiliation with the Republican Party was, I am sure, purely coincidental. At any rate, prospects were so bad in Georgia for a Republican that history tells us he left Savannah at the age of five.

I have warned our speaker about his audience. Now let me give him a word of warning about Savannah itself. You may have heard of Chatham Artillery Punch, which not only possesses the most potent kick of any libation known to humanity but at the same time leaves one with a magnificent obsession of grandeur. Admiral Dewey, a good Republican, visited Savannah in 1900 and, tradition tells us, attended a banquet such as this one at which Chatham Artillery Punch flowed merrily. The next day he woke up and announced his candidacy for president of the United States on the Democratic ticket. We have, however, taken such good care today of the distinguished senator from Massachusetts that I am sure Truman, Eisenhower and Taft need have no fears of any announcement from him tomorrow.

We have connections here, too, with New England, of which you may not be aware, Senator. Thirty miles south sits the little village of Midway, a place to which many New Englanders migrated long years ago. Some time before the turn of the eighteenth century a certain Dr. Holmes, a minister of the gospel, presided over the congregation for several months. He and Mrs. Holmes then returned to Massachusetts, where a few months later their son Oliver Wendell Holmes was born. The birth of this baby, who was to gain fame as something of an autocrat while eating breakfast, proves that New England claims credit for many fine things conceived in Georgia.

Our speaker derives from a line of forebears distinguished and unique even for the Commonwealth of Massachusetts. Eight former governors are numbered among his ancestors. He is the tenth Saltonstall in direct succession, we are told, who attended Harvard University – a tribute to the tenacity, if not to the discrimination of the Saltonstalls. He was a leading athlete at Harvard. He served as a first lieutenant in the first World War. He became a lawyer. Later he entered politics and was a member of the legislature. He served as speaker of the General Assembly of Massachusetts for four years. In 1938 he was elected governor of that Commonwealth and two years later when President Roosevelt carried the state by 137,000 votes, he was returned to office by a sizeable majority. In 1944, by a 400,000 majority, he was elected to the United States Senate. He has served in that august body with great distinction. It is a peculiar pleasure, ladies and gentlemen, to present to this magnificent and friendly audience, a great American – the distinguished Senator from Massachusetts, the Honorable Leverett Saltonstall.

Diary of An Innocent Abroad

(Final luncheon of a European touring group, Paris, October 14, 1962.)

Sept. 27: Leave Idlewild for London on Alitalia with accomodations in airship steerage. Sleep like top (tops don't sleep).

Sept. 28: Alitalia very fast. Before we are registered at Strand Palace Hotel most of our baggage is back at New York. Sleep until tea time and then have tea for two at Savoy Hotel – "high tea," 1 pound, 2 shillings.

Sept. 29: Absorb much English culture today, especially Streptococcus culture. Visit Westminister Abbey. Evidently there is no cemetery nearby as they bury people under the floor as well as in the walls. See Buckingham Palace. It has a fence around it with spikes put there by Queen Victoria to keep Wally Simpson from getting in. Served later to keep Princess Margaret from getting out.

In afternoon take bus trip to St. Paul's and to Tower of London. Tower good place to put old wives. Visit Old Curiosity Shop. Most curious thing about it is why they take us there.

Sept. 30: Visit Shakespeare country by bus. Stop enroute at Oxford. Do not see changing of the guards as it took place today in Oxford, Mississippi. Visit Ann Hathaway's house in Stratford. Shakespeare's room reminds me of our accommodations at Strand

Palace Hotel. Visit Warwick Castle but Earl of Warwick out making kings, or maybe a queen.

Oct. 1: Goodbye Piccadilly! Hello Zurich! From there go by bus to Lucerne. Sit on balcony of Hotel Balances and start on bottle of Georgia Chianti (Early Times). By time I finish it Swiss scenery look very rosy, indeed.

Oct. 2: Scale Mount Pilatus. It has cable car just like Stone Mountain but lacks a Confederate monument. Ladies spend good part of day at quaint Swiss village they call Bucherer.

Oct. 3: Motor to Milan through beautiful lake country. There we see the Duomo Cathedral, La Scala (but not La Callas), da Vinci's Last Supper and, as our guide said, "et cetera, et cetera, et cetera." Travel by train to Venice. Get in funny row boat and paddle over to Luna Hotel. Venice good example of how a city can overcome parking problem.

Oct. 4: See the sights and smell the aromas of Venice. Impressed by St. Mark's Square – it is only place in Europe where I can smoke a cigar without Margaret threatening to go back to my mother-in-law. Pick out expensive emerald ring for her but unable to conclude purchase; Venetians never heard of lay-away plan. Visit Bridge of Sighs. It gets name from fact that while wives go shopping husbands stand on it and sigh.

Oct. 5: Travel to Florence. Ladies very interested in Florentine art. They attend Leather School most of day. Stay at Astoria Hotel in quiet part of city. Only noise at night is automobiles, trucks, busses, scooters and men yelling "Bambino." Italians must think Babe Ruth playing in World Series.

Oct. 6: Visit Uffizi Gallery, Acadmey Museum and Pitti Palace, all of which are rated "first-class" by Fielding. See paintings by Michelangelo, da Vinci, Botticelli, Raphael, Titian and Tintoretto. Renaissance artists compare not unfavorably with Whistler, Winslow

Homer, Norman Rockwell and Grandma Moses. American painters, however, are more up-to-date. They have better equipment, too. Poor Italian artists often had nothing to paint on but ceilings and walls.

Also see much fine sculpture in Florence. Evidentaly Italy was as full of chiselers in Renaissance days as it is now. See Michelangelo's statue of David. It is the biggest indoor statue we've seen so far. The work is in the heroic style as little David is preparing to fight Goliath single-handed. We are really catching on to Renaissance art.

Oct. 7: Travel by bus to Rome via Perugia. Stop at hill-top town of Assisi where we see Basilica of St. Francis. Not impressed by fact that St. Francis's bones lie there. We got fossils in my church back home that walk and talk.

Oct. 8: Rome was not built in a day but we just about see it in one. Not too hard as the city consists largely of basilicas, ruins, fountains, side-walk cafes and museums where one finds the inevitable statuary and painting. See the Colosseum where they fed Protestants to the lions. Visit the Roman Forum at night. Impressed by lighting system installed by the early emperors. Circus Maximus is closed for season but see the next best thing – Rome's taxi drivers. They are indirect descendants of Roman charioteers.

Oct. 9: Take in the Borghese Gallery where we see Bernini's statue of Apollo chasing Daphne. She is changing into a laurel tree and has bark on her shins and twigs on her hands. All I can say is Daphne's got funny-looking limbs.

Ectasy becomes agony when ladies cannot see Michelangelo's alfrescoes in the Vatican. The Pope selected this day, of all days, to convene the first Ecumenical Council in 92 years. However, we get to see the top of the Pope's mitre as he walks in procession in magnificent St. Peter's.

Oct. 10: Take all-day and most all-night trip by bus. Visit Pompeii. This town was very backward for many years but is showing big economic improvement. It is still much in need of repair, however. See room in the House of Vettii to which women under seventy not admitted. Have lunch at pretty hotel near Salerno. Apparently the hotel is the center of Europe's music box industry. Drive 500 miles to Amalfi. The drive is a four-lane highway – for motorcycles. Stop at Cassina at night and see Lorenzo's Last Supper; that is to say, the last supper they'll ever see Lawrence eat there.

Oct. 11: Drop three coins in Trevi Fountain. Then wish I hadn't. They about only coins I got left. Make close study of Michelangelo's celebrated statue of Moses. Not nearly as big as his David.

Oct. 12: Fly to Paris. Take bus trip in afternoon. See, among other sights, the Place de la Concorde. The French are great imitators. The fountain there is a copy of the one in Forsyth Park at Savannah. Take in the Louvre. It has more paintings than any museum we've seen so far. We average twenty masterpieces a minute. I would classify most of the paintings as non-Impressionist. However, Mona Lisa is very impressive. Her eyes intrigued me more than her smile. They remind me of Margaret's. Stand way over on left of crowd and Mona is looking straight at me. Move over to the right and she's still got her eye on me. Go to center of group and stand close to Patsy Martin, and now Mona sees me better than ever.

See celebrated "Wingless Victory" by Sammy Thrace. Also study the famous bust of Venus de Milo. At night go to Follies Bergère and look at modern busts. They much more interesting.

Oct. 13: Bad headache. Evidently eye strain. Go on another sightseeing tour. The Seine is not nearly as big as the Savannah. However, we got no Left Bank. The Goths built some fine cathedrals. However, the exterior of Notre Dame is marred by many very disagreeable creatures they call gargoyles. In my opinion, the early Italian architects were better than the early French architects as the latter had to build flying buttresses to prop up their cathedrals.

On the other hand, the Pantheon in Paris is better constructed than the Pantheon in Rome which has a big hole in the roof.

Visit Napoleon's Tomb. Gaze at it and say to myself: "*Sic semper tyrannis! Sic transit gloria mundi!* Sick of mausoleums!"

Oct. 14: Visit Versailles. It is too much in the Louis-Quatorze style for me. See bed in which Louis the Fifteenth slept. Also see bed in which Madame de Pompadour slept. Same bed!

Oct. 15: Evidently the President of France wants to make sure that we leave his country, for hundreds of gendarmes line our route to airport. 1.30 PM – Westward ho! *Au revoir*, Gay Paree!

Our Colonial Foremothers

(Georgia Society of Colonial Dames banquet, Savannah, April 11, 1956.)

I have heard that this is a very serious group and am told you don't welcome levity in any form. I once saw a few lines about the Colonial Dames which perhaps are the source of my impression of your austerity. The limerick I heard went like this:

The DAR-lings chattered like starlings,
Reciting their ancestors' names,
While cold and aloof
And full of reproof
Sat the Colonial Dames.

If that is going to be your attitude, let me tell you what I think of you here and now:

If you Dames sit proud and aloof,
I'll say nothing in your behoof;
For with equal abhorrence
You are looked on by Lawrence
Who fears only one Dame's reproof.

I will have you Colonial Dames know that I have spoken before equally exclusive organizations. Take, for example, the Daughters of Runnymede – or better than that, *you* take them. They are composed of the direct female descendants of the barons who browbeat King John into granting the Magna Carta. They are still just as formidable.

Some day I hope to get an invitation to speak to the Order of the First Crusade. It is composed of the Descendants of the Seven Knights of the First Crusade which took place in the year 1096. Now, here is a really exclusive group. At least one would suppose so. However, under a literal interpretation of the Malthusian Law of the increase of population faster than the means of subsistence, I estimate that some 50 million women are now eligible for membership in the Descendants of the Seven Knights.

"Genealogy" has been defined as "An account of one's descent from an ancestor who did not particularly care to trace his own." I would have you Dames know that I, too, have ancestors and, like you, am a descendant. In fact, my family has been descending for hundreds of years. I only hope I can begat myself a line of ascendants.

My first ancestor came over on the *Mayflower* with William the Conqueror. The immigration laws weren't very strict in those days. He was a veteran of the War of the Roses, or as we call it down here the War Between the Roses. What he was running away from I don't know. We have traced him but apparently the English authorities couldn't.

I think it was Edmund Burke who said: "Let us put our footsteps in the paths of our fathers for there we cannot err and cannot stray." Now this has always seemed rather silly to me – this business of going around and looking for your forefathers' footprints to put your feet in. Someday I will be a forefather myself and I certainly wouldn't like my posterity tracking me down. I don't want anybody following my paths – dead or alive. The idea of being a shadow is repugnant enough, but the thought of being a shadowed shadow is absolutely repulsive.

New Perspectives on Early Georgia

(This "pop" version of Georgia history was first used in 1962, and in succeeding years it was repeated with slight variations in several cities.)

I

Many moons ago an Indian village called Yamacraw was located on the blue and unpolluted waters of the Isondiga River where it bends like a great bow around the tall bluff eighteen miles from the shining big sea water.

Yamacraw was Paradise and Utopia. All day the Indian braves hunted and fished and canoed. On Sundays they watched the Redskins play the Braves at lacrosse. The Braves always lost. Meanwhile, their squaws knew their place was in the wigwam where they had to mind their little squawlers. It was a halcyon era. There were no papoose sitters, no little leaguers, no den mothers (except female bears) and no disease except whooping cough and it came from too much whooping.

Then one February day nearly 250 years ago things suddenly changed. A startled cry ran through the Indian village. "The Red Coats are coming! The Red Coats are coming! Run for your ax-handles."

One hundred and twelve English settlers under James Edward Oglethorpe had crossed the Atlantic on the Good Ship *Ann* to establish a new colony in the New World. Up in New England they boast of their descent from those who came over on the Mayflower and landed on Plymouth Rock. (I wish the Rock had landed on the Pilgrim fathers!) But nobody is ever heard to brag about their ancestors coming over on the *Ann*. The trouble was her passenger list. The colonists were debtors. Think of that! They had come to settle in Georgia because they were unable to settle back home. They lived two hundred years too soon. They should have waited until charge cards and consumer credit came along and everybody's broke.

Now the head of the Yamacraw nation in those days was wise old Tomochichi. He had seen many Indian summers and I suppose just as many Indian Springs. He gave the English settlers a royal welcome. Apparently Tomochichi wasn't at all class-conscious.

But there were voices of discord and bickering in Yamacraw even in that day. Some of the redskins were dead-set against bringing newcomers into the village. The spokesman of the dissident faction was the medicine man. Naturally, he was prejudiced. As a member of AMMA (which, of course, was the American Medicine Mens' Association) he knew what socialized medicine had done to his profession in Great Britain.

The witch doctor strongly advised against letting any immigrants into Georgia. His idea about immigration was expressed in those beautiful lines inscribed on the great totem pole these native Americans raised at the edge of the river. On top was a wooden Indian with his arm and hand toward the Atlantic like a traffic cop's. "Don't give us your tired, your poor . . . the wretched refuse of your teeming shore."

An open door policy was strenuously protested by the medicine man. "Chief, we need to tighten up our immigration laws", he said. "Let's keep Georgia red!"

Tomochichi shook his head. "We need tourists," he said. "Yamacraw got more drop-outs than it got drop-ins. Them Fennimore Cooper injuns up on the Mohawk, they is nothing but poor red trash. But they 'way ahead of us industrially. All we got is little plant that make pottery. And even it gone to pot. Our gross national product so gross we can't even give it away. Ain't no market in the world common enough for Yamacraw to barter in. Yamacraw is Number One Backward Nation in world."

"Yamacraw not backward nation," protested the medicine man, "we just underdeveloped country. Chief, these paleface no different from Pilgrim fathers. First thing they do when they land on Plymouth Rock is fall on knees. Then they get up and fall on aborigines."*

(Please bear with me. I have had to translate dead Creek scrolls into the modern Geechee that I speak and it isn't easy.)

The chief's face now took on a stony look which wasn't hard for a Stone Age Indian's face to do. The medicine man also grew red in the face but it wasn't noticeable either. "Why not stall the English off until we get further along with our SEATO Program?" he asked. (SEATO, of course, stood for the "Southeastern Arrow and Tomahawk Organization".)

In reply Tomochichi spoke sad words, "SEATO, it fall apart! The only ally we got left is the Upper Creeks and they is even lower than us Lower Creeks. How us Yamacraws going to fight when we got no four-lane warpaths around here?"

The medicine man then protruded his jaw. He lowered his brow and spoke eloquent words: "We must defend our village whatever the cost may be. We shall fight on our bluff and in the forest. We shall never surrender."

The chief looked at his medicine man like he was crazy. "Doc," he said, "you is not only a plagiarist but you got the phoniest English accent I ever heard."

"I think I go up now," added the chief "and have summit conference with Oglethorpe. "Bluff good place for summit meeting," muttered the medicine man, "but pow-wow always end up in kow-tow by us poor Injuns."

At this critical moment in Georgia's history, Tomochichi saw Mary Musgrove passing by. Mary was a half-breed and was the niece of the famous Emperor Brim. Her Indian name was Coosaponakee. She was married to an Englishman who ran a trading post at Yamacraw.

"You my advisor on foreign affairs," said Tomochichi, "you

*Anonymous.

sure have had enough of them to be expert. What you think about this, Coosaponakee?"

"Don't trust that squaw!" the medicine man warned. "You know why she wear that thick petticoat? She think us dumb Injuns not see through her. She nothing but Indian Love Call girl."

Tomochichi paid no attention. Coosaponakee replied that Oglethorpe was the friend of the red man and that he was noted in England for his philanthropy.

"Oglethorpe is the friend of the red man," echoed Tomochichi. "He is heap big philanthropist. But me even be bigger one. If it "blessed to be an English giver, then it twice blessed to be an Indian giver."

So all the Yamacraws went down on River Street to greet the palefaces. There they drank firewater together. Then they joined in singing Yamacraw's national anthem in celebration of the new treaty with the English:

I'm glad I lib in de lan' of Geechee
Huntin' ground of Tomochichi,
Wanta stay, wanta stay, wanta stay,
Geecheeland.

Oh, I glad I am a Geechee
Whoopee! Whoopee!
In Yamacraw I'll take my stand
To live and die a Geechee
A low, a low, a low-down
Southern Geechee.

II

It wasn't long before the English settlers spread southward down the coast of Georgia. They built Fort Frederica on St. Simons Island, which was only ninety miles from St. Augustine. The establishment of this military installation made a confrontation with the Spanish inevitable. One day a Spanish coast guard vessel stopped an English brig off St. Augustine. The Spaniards claimed she was engaged in spying. Actually she was on a legitimate mission – smuggling. The captain of the English ship was Thomas Jenkins. As a warning to the British, the Spaniards cut off one of his ears. Then with customary Spanish courtesy they handed it back to him.

Captain Jenkins pickled the ear in vinegar and carried it to London. He appeared before Parliament and made the famous speech which begins, "Friends, Britons, countrymen, lend me an ear." The members of Parliament looked into the jar of preserves and were shocked. Why, I don't know. The ear was not half as rotten as their "Rotten Boroughs".

The Greeks and the Trojans went to war over a pretty woman's face – probably the only war in history where the common soldier understood what he was really fighting for. But the "War of Jenkins' Ear," which now commenced, is the only war ever fought over somebody's ear. Usually it is someone's big mouth.

In 1742 the Spanish invaded Georgia and landed on St. Simons Island. These Spaniards were smart hombres. They saw the wonderful vacation possibilities of the Golden Islands. If they were beaten, they could always retire to Jekyll Island as a last resort.

Fort Frederica was defended by Oglethorpe's Regiment and a unit of Scotch Highlanders from Darien, Georgia. Until almost the last minute, however, they seemed no match for the well-equipped Spaniards. The British finally tried a desperate maneuver which resulted in the decisive Battle of Bloody Marsh. The defeated Spaniards decided to pass up Jekyll Island as their retirement home, however, because they found that neither J. P. Morgan nor William Rockefeller had any port or sherry in his cellar. And that's the inside story of the Battle of Bloody Marsh and why we speak broken English instead of Spanish.

After the threat of domination by Spain was removed – now that America was no longer endangered by Ponce de Leon, Pizarro and Cortes – the colony got on the high road to economic success. The Royal Chief Justice of Georgia, Anthony Stokes, would write that under the King's government Georgia was "one of the most free and happy countries in the world – justice was regularly and impartially administered – oppression was unknown – the taxes levied on the subject were trifling – and every man that had industry became opulent . . . such a rapid progress in population, agriculture, and commerce . . . no other country ever equalled in so short a time!"

But history teaches us that Utopias soon become Hell. The colonists got mad about the Stamp Tax. Why our forefathers objected so much to "Taxation without representation" beats me. We would still be British subjects if they had ever realized what "Taxation with Representation" would be like. George the Third thought the colonists were revolting. They thought he was revolting. So they went to war. The Colony got its independence. With it, prosperity disappeared.

How Georgia and the Southern states got back on their economic feet brings us to the story of the wife of General Nathanael Greene. As a reward, for his brillant feats in the Revolution, Georgia granted the general a plantation up the Savannah River called "Mulberry Grove." His wife, Katy, was one of the most attractive women of her day or of any other day.

Jealous females said of her that "she had no more gravity than an air balloon." Mrs. Greene knew nothing about the Law of Gravity but she knew a lot about the Law of Levity. She seemed to have a particular attraction for Revolutionary generals. Besides her husband, there were LaFayette, Wadsworth, "Light Horse" Harry Lee and Anthony Wayne. General Wayne lived next to "Mulberry Grove." He fell under her spell. There was much gossip. Women said that she should be banished from society forever. Her husband said that he had been "tickled infinitely . . . while the two of them flirted desperately," but actually Nathanael didn't like it one bit and he told Anthony as much. General Wayne didn't like being called down and that is where he got his name "Mad."

During his southern tour in 1791 President Washington stopped by "Mulberry Grove" to call on his old friend. He wrote in his diary, "I asked Mrs. Greene how she did." Now this is the greatest presidential understatement of all time. Talk about White House credibility gaps! President Washington almost didn't get to Savannah for the reception in his honor that evening.

One day in the year 1793 a young man who had a bent for popular mechanics dropped by "Mulberry Grove" on his way to South Carolina where he had engaged himself to be a tutor. He stopped by for a few days and he stayed six months. That was the way Mrs. Greene was – she was anything but "Katy Bar the Door."

This young man from Connecticut had been at "Mulberry Grove" only a few days when he invented a new type of frame or tambour for holding the widow Greene's needlework. Then she really cound needle. And she did. She insisted that her guest try to solve an economic problem at Mulberry Grove. In fact, the whole South had the same one. Millions of acres of land were good for nothing but raising cotton. But you couldn't get the seed out of upland cotton except by laborious hand work. One person could produce only two pounds of clean lint a day, so firmly was the green seed immeshed in the short fibre.

Katy was then in the Indian summer of her charms, but there is no doubt that the young New Englander was attracted to her. He decided to accept the challenge of finding a way to get the seeds out of the widow's cotton. He made up his mind that he would prove his fibre by improving her fibre. It isn't the first time a prominent woman's future has figured prominently in history.

At first he seemed to get nowhere. In fact, he was so frustrated he took to drink. He used to sit on the veranda overlooking the river with a Tom Collins by his side and muse over the problem of inventing a contraption to get seeds out of cotton. One afternoon a servant started to removed his unfinished drink. Whereupon the New Englander gave utterance to that immortal line, "Take your cotton-picking hands off my gin!"

Gin! Cotton! Cotton Gin. Eureka! And that is the inside story of how Eli Whitney came to invent the cotton gin!

III

As a result of the invention, the South began to prosper as never before. The cotton planters built beautiful colonial mansions and sat on the piazza most of the day fanning themselves. In the evening they sipped juleps among the tulips and at night under the moon-lit magnolias they sang "Way Down Upon the Suwannee River" and "Old White Joe."

Why this idyllic pattern of life worried the people up North so much is beyond me. We weren't bothering nobody. And all we asked was that nobody bother us. The truth was the North was jealous of the Utopia Eli Whitney's invention helped bring about. Southerners were living in state. The North wanted us to live in a nation. As Abraham Lincoln said: "This government cannot endure permanently half slave and half free. It must be all for free or there'll be a free-for-all."

So we went to war. Old Abe dispatched one Union general after another down here to conquer us. The poor Confederates just wore themselves out beating Yankee generals. They "whupped" all except the last two on the roster – Grant and Sherman.

At that point this History comes to a close. The sequel of Appomattox is well known. All I can add is that sometimes I wish General Longstreet had come up on time at Gettysburg on a warm July morning long, long ago. Things might be a little different today.

History As It Might Have Been

If Longstreet Had Come Up At Gettysburg

(Atlanta Historical Society, "Celebration of the Eighty-Fourth Anniversary of the Surrender of Washington, D.C.," Atlanta, October 25, 1947.)

A locust-swarm of historians is devouring America's past. Scholars and students probe every nook and cranny of the origin, growth and development of our institutions. The major as well as minor figures of American history have been examined under countless historical microscopes. Every facet of the past, no matter how insignificant, is the prey of the historical writer. Almost no figure is too obscure for a doctoral dissertation. The presses of the country are groaning with the weight of memoirs, biography and history. The land is crawling with the historical novelist. One can scarcely write on a phase or figure of American history without dealing with the winnowings of another's research.

Confronted with the problem of so little that is fresh or new in history, I should like to undertake a departure from the conventional. I propose an experiment that may lead, for aught one knows, to a new era in historical approach. To the jaded historian I offer a new and wider horizon of research and endeavor – a field in which one is not restrained by the actualities of the past.

There is of course nothing new or novel in a treatment of the "ifs" and "might-have-beens" of history. To some extent they are inescapable in any adequate appraisal of men or events. Perhaps it is true, as many will say, that to deal with them is an idle and futile, an even silly, pastime. The trouble with the "might-have-been" school of history is that the average historian is so preoccupied with the past as it really was that he has never developed a good technique of dealing with the things that might have happened. One may scoff at such an approach to history as being wholly imaginative, even nonsensical, but the simple truth is that much of history was purely chance – the present being in many respects the end product of the fortuities of the past. My answer to such critics is that by applying the true historical method to what did *not* take place in the past we can understand far better and see in truer perspective the things which *did* occur. My thesis is that things as they are can be better comprehended by an understanding of what they well might have been.

As an initial experiment in this neo-historiological technique I should like to use as a testing ground the Battle of Gettysburg with the "might-have-beens" and "ifs" of General Longstreet's role in it, the title of this paper being: "If Longstreet had come up at Gettysburg; a History of the American States since July 2, 1863." Perhaps in the mirror of the might-have-been we may see reflected the vanities, faults and condescensions of the present-day enemies of the South. Perhaps such an approach to history may permit something in the way of a reply to the strident and tireless minority which ceaselessly makes war against the South's pattern of life and endlessly berates and belittles us – a reply, however, if I may say it, in which I hope slander can be answered with satire, hatred with humor and ire with irony.

Before setting out on this little adventure in the realm of historical fantasy it is necessary to review what actually occurred at Gettysburg and what actually followed Lee's great defeat there. My only excuse for rehearsing a tale so little-pleasing to Southern ears is that it is an indispensable prelude to history as it might have read if General Longstreet had come up on one July morning in the year 1863. . .

In the spring of 1863 the South was a beleaguered fortress. Hooker's army was threatening Richmond. At Vicksburg, General Grant's forces gnawed at the innards of the Confederacy. To relieve the Confederate capital as well as to secure adequate supplies for the Army the Southern leaders determined to carry the war into enemy territory. For that purpose General Lee had available the Army of Northern Virginia, a superb fighting force of 75,000 tried veterans in which he reposed the highest confidence, believing that even without the lamented Stonewall Jackson it could accomplish almost anything. The victory at Chancellorsville had raised the spirit of his men to the highest pitch. Against this background the invasion of the North in the Summer of '63 was planned. Essentially the Pennsylvania Campaign was to be of a diversionary rather than a decisive nature. But there were high hopes that the trans-Potomac venture would lend real encouragement to the peace party in the North which was no inconsiderable or inarticulate one. The quarry was an even larger one in some eyes. It is recorded by one witness that General Lee, pointing to the little town of Gettysburg on a map, had remarked: "Hereabout we shall probably meet the enemy and fight a great battle, and if God gives us victory, the war will be over and we shall achieve the recognition of our independence."

But an ominous diversity of opinion existed on Lee's staff. General James Longstreet had opposed the campaign from the first, insisting that if undertaken at all it should be defensive in nature and that no general engagement should be fought. This attitude permeated his actions in the campaign that followed.

We know how Lee's grey-clad divisions crossed the Potomac in June, marched into the rolling farm-lands of Pennsylvania and converged on the little village of Gettysburg. We have heard how the cavalry forces under General Stuart which had been detached on June 24th failed to maintain communication with Lee's main army, depriving the Confederate commander of adequate knowledge of the movements of the Federals. It is an old story how the Army of Northern Virginia stumbled upon Meade's advance units at Gettysburg late on July 1st, 1863, and how in the first shock of battle victory rode with the Confederacy. We know that Lee planned on the next day to seize the fish-hook ridges commanding the town to the south and southeast which were then only weakly held by Meade's forces. We have been told that on the early morning of July 2nd the Union troops on the ridges near Cemetery Hill which Longstreet was expected to attack were still not formidable in number. From able students of the campaign we learn that the early hours of that day passed while Longstreet dallied and Lee impatiently watched more and more Federal troops arrive. Nine, ten o'clock – General Longstreet was not in position. Eleven o'clock – noon ("Whatever *can* detain Longstreet?") – the early afternoon hours pass, and the Confederate attack is still not mounted. The green of the ridges has become blue. Not until after five does word reach Lee that Longstreet is in position. The Confederate lines advance. Ground is gained at fearful cost. But when night closes in, the battered soldiers of the Confederacy had failed to dislodge the enemy from the hills.

The rest of the chapter we know all too well – how on the 3rd the long grey lines of the Confederacy rolled up to the ridges occupied by the enemy and then rolled back. Stephen Vincent Benét has expressed it beautifully in *John Brown's Body*:

The South came
And Pickett came,
And the end came,
And the grass comes
And the wind blows
Over the bronze book
Over the bronze men,
Over the grown grass,
And the wind says,
"Long ago, Long Ago."

From Gettysburg the grey line went back to Virginia; back to the siege of Richmond; to gradual attrition, and the bitter end. With the collapse of the Confederacy came the long hard days of Northern vengeance; Reconstruction; sectional poverty and political proscription; economic vassalism and provincial status with the Southern people the eternal whipping-boy and scape-goat of the dominant section of the Union. All these things may not have been the actual consequence of Gettysburg – perhaps they would have come about in all events; yet, in the chain of causation of human events, that they have the appearance of being the result and aftermath of the South's defeat in that great battle who will deny?

These things we learn from history. But what the history books do not tell the reader is what the South and America might have been and would be today, had General Longstreet come up at the right time on that fateful day long, long ago. Applying the true historical method, let us pursue the possibilities of that supposition. In the manner of non-partisan Northern historians, shall we say of the James Ford Rhodes school, I offer the following brief history of the American States since the early morning of July 2, 1863, when Lee's veterans stormed the hills that overlook the historic little Pennsylvania village.

. . . .

Stirred by their successes of the afternoon of July 1st the slumbers of Lee's men were broken by dreams of the morrow. What would it bring? What would be the result of a day so pregnant with import to the future of the Confederate States of America, to the North American continent, nay to the very world itself? Would there be two republics in America? Would Washington or Richmond be the American capital? In their bivouacs Confederate wags drew lusty laughter when they predicted that after July 2nd fried chicken would be the national dish.

At the council of war that night General Longstreet still disapproved of a general offensive engagement. But Lee, pointing over toward Cemetery Ridge, toward Little Round Top and Culp's Hill (names soon to become so ominous in the textbooks of the North), had declared "If the enemy is there, we must attack him" and Longstreet had yielded. Returning to his command, he ordered the First Corps brought up as rapidly as possible. That night beneath the pale moon that lit the wheatfields of Pennsylvania the columns of Hood and McLaws moved up. The coming of dawn on the 2nd found the grey battalions shaping for battle along the slopes from which they were to advance. It was barely 9 o'clock when the thunder of Longstreet's guns near Cemetery

Hill sounded the signal for the attack. Within an hour, after a bloody engagement, Ewell was in possession of Culp's Hill and the Peach Orchard. Lee had correctly surmised that Cemetery Ridge had not been reinforced. But at Devil's Den and Little and Big Round Top there was tenacious resistance. However, the grip of the Federals along the ridge was broken. By noon the battle flags of the Confederacy dominated the rising ground southeast of Gettysburg. The Union forces had been shaken. However, the full weight of Meade's army had still not been brought to bear against Lee. East of the Ridges the roads were choked with blue columns moving up from the South.

For the Union the situation was discouraging but not irreparable – at least so Meade conceived. It was late in the day before the counter-attack was ready. The 5th and 7th corps of his army struck hard at the Confederate positions along Cemetery Ridge. In the gathering dusk, the blue lines sought again and again to retrieve the ground which Longstreet had won that morning. The desperation with which they fought in the deepening gloom of a July afternoon is part of the folklore of American history. But when the sun set over the bloody field of Gettysburg the Army of the Potomac was badly hurt. It had suffered 20,000 casualties besides thousands of prisoners. At great cost the South had held the hills, but held them Lee had. What would Meade do? To retreat upon Baltimore, Philadelphia or Washington after a crushing defeat in Pennsylvania would be to give such aid and comfort to Vallandigham and the clamorous Copperhead party – would be to raise the prestige of the Confederacy with England and France so much – that withdrawal seemed out of question. Yet equally fatal was it to continue the attack on the morrow. On the other hand, what would or could Lee do? Were his battle-weary divisions able to follow up their advantage? Would Gettysburg prove to be another Manassas – another Seven Days fighting, where the fruits of total victory would be tantalizingly snatched from the Confederacy?

Meanwhile late on the 2nd the wandering Jeb Stuart had arrived with four cavalry brigades. Pickett's Division had also come up, fresh for the fray. Meade had withdrawn his line about a mile to the east. From an all-night staff meeting he emerged from his headquarters at daybreak on the 3rd to hear the fateful roll of guns near the great Baltimore Turnpike toward the southeast. Galloping up, an excited courier reported that Stuart had crossed the left flank of the Union forces during the night and was at Taneytown, supported by Confederate infantry, ominously threatening the Federal rear. The order for a general retreat was given. The roads fanning eastward from Gettysburg were clogged with troop trains. Withdrawal was a difficult maneuver.

As soon as the retreat of the Union forces became a certainty, Lee's troops debouched from the hills, falling upon the remnants of the Third and Sixth corps which were assigned to protect the rear of Meade's retreating forces. General E. P. Alexander's artillery wrought havoc in their ranks. Stuart and his cavalry, fighting desperately, delayed the retreat of the Union forces to the southeast. Sickles' Corps, still fairly intact, was forced to cross rough country toward the York Road only to find that Early's Division had already fought its way down it well to the east. By four o'clock disorganization had become chaos; by five, rout had become disaster. General Meade himself was taken prisoner. Blenheim had been re-enacted. It was Waterloo all over. The proud Army of the Potomac was no more. Remnants would escape to Hanover, but not to fight again as an effective military force. Of a magnificent army of 80,000 men, 35,000 were dead or wounded. Another 25,000 were prisoners of Lee. Enormous stores of military equipment had fallen into Confederate hands.

But Manassas had been a rout and the North had returned more determined than ever; from disaster at Fredericksburg the Union had rebounded in still greater strength. A great battle had been fought in Pennsylvania; a stupendous defeat inflicted on the enemy. Yet could an army which had sustained such losses as Lee's be humanly expected to take advantage of its victory before Union replacements took the field?

Lee acted with matchless decision and promptness. The seat of Union arrogance, Washington, D.C., must be the main goal; to strangle the West, the second. To divide his forces in the heart of the enemy's country, under other conditions, might be reckless folly. Yet that is what General Lee did. Already the Baltimore and Ohio Railroad and the Chesapeake & Ohio Canal had been cut by the Confederacy. The entire Second Corps with Early's, Johnson's and Rodes' divisions, was hurried northward to disrupt communication between the East and West through the railroad centers at Harrisburg and Williamsport.

The North seethed with fear. Rioting was universal. Baltimore was seized by Southern sympathizers. In Washington "panic" was a mild term for the state of mind of the politicasters who since 1861 had polluted the once-sacred precincts of the capital of the American federation. A strong series of fortifications, almost square-shaped, surrounded Washington City where a prudent commander had insisted that General Hooker not be allowed to deplete the garrison. Lincoln promptly ordered all Union troops in Virginia and West Virginia to fall back on Washington. The Northern capital was invested by Lee. The long siege commenced. By mid-September the defenders had been reduced to a diet of horsemeat, with newspapers being printed on wallpaper. Even more ominous in Washington than the meat shortage was this scarcity of newsprint. The curtailment of the Appendix to the *Congressional Globe* caused grave unrest among the Union solons to whom the loss of the privilege of extending their remarks was a sacrifice almost beyond words.

Two weeks before the fall of Washington President Lincoln was captured by a Confederate scouting party near Martinsburg. This well-known episode has been the subject of exaggeration by some historical writers. Undoubtedly Mr. Lincoln availed himself of the "Underground Railway" in attempting to escape from the besieged capital But there is no factual basis for the oft-repeated canard that the President was recognized through his disguise of a runaway slave by an alert Confederate private who had once seen his profile on a unit of currency. In the party with Lincoln was the notorious Thad Stevens – an appropriate commentary on the character of a man who had grandiosely announced to Congress that he would die in the rubble of the Capitol before he would suffer capture by the Confederates.

No historian of the period can pass over this bizarre chapter without contemplating for a moment the strange career of Mr. Lincoln. This gaunt and lonely man, the victim of his incompetent generals, must be numbered among the more tragic figures of history. Groping from mistake to mistake, attempting to substitute patience and droll stories for decision and energy – Lincoln is the very symbol of Northern blundering. He would live out his years quietly on the prairies, rationalizing his mistakes, and arguing in fine-spun theory the archaic notion that a Federal Union which had been utterly perverted from the ideas of the Founding Fathers was indissoluble and perpetual.

On October 25th, 1863 the city of Washington, hoping to the bitter end for relief from Grant which never came, was surrendered after a defense with few parallels in history for tenaciousness. We celebrate today the anniversary on which General Halleck unconditionally surrendered the city as the strains of "Dixie" and the rebel yell of "Lee's Miserables" echoed among the ruins along Pennsylvania Avenue. Fittingly enough, the ceremony took place aboard the famous Confederate man-of-war *Alabama*, which had just completed an epic cruise to home waters for that purpose.

Meanwhile the isolated Confederate forces in Pennsylvania had maintained their grip on the approaches to the West. Despite vicious attacks by the new militia levies called up in the North, they had held the vital line of the Susquehanna. Grant had been forced to fall back from Vicksburg to the Ohio on account of inadequate supplies. Rosecrans evacuated Tennessee. Other invading units were left to wither on the vine. (Alas, alas, for Margaret Mitchell and the Atlanta Historical Society! Sherman never saw Peachtree Creek.) The recognition of the Confederate States by England sounded the death knell of the blockade of Southern ports . . . but the North was still far from subdued.

The release of the border states – Tennessee, Maryland and Kentucky – from the "despot's heel" meant an important addition to the South's war potential. For the coming invasion of the upper North every able-bodied man in the Confederacy had been mustered into service. The astute Davis and his cabinet realized all-too-well that as long as the devil-disciples of Abolitiondom held sway in the cesspool that was New England the Confederacy could never be secure. On New Year's Day, 1864, Lee's legions, now one-hundred strong, crossed the Delaware. It was on February 22nd of that year that President Davis delivered his famous address at Gettysburg commemorating the South's great victory there, beginning with the lines so well known to every school boy:

> *Gettysburg will never be forgotten among free peoples for its eternal lesson that no matter in what vast armaments Aggression may accouter itself, it can never break the bulwarks of freedom and humanity as long as brave men live and dare to die.*

New York City had been expected to offer a fierce, perhaps fatal, resistance to Lee's veterans. But the South was to find many friends there. To the Tammany politicians the entrance of soldiers of Democracy into New York spelled the redemption of that metropolis from a fate worse than death. To the economic nabobs of the city who had fattened so long on trade and the tariff, peaceable surrender at least meant the sparing of their mansions from the torch and cannon. Nevertheless, one group of die-hard millionaires, ordering their carriagemen and valets into the fray, offered a stout resistance which ended only when their spirit was broken by the capture of their stronghold – the Union League Club. On April 1, 1864, the Stars and Bars of the Confederacy floated over Times Square. The surrender of Brooklyn was delayed for several days by the difficulty the Confederates experienced in finding any officials in that city who could conduct the negotiations in English.

Longstreet's celebrated March to the Sea commenced the following month. Silhouetted by the bonfires of the villages, farms and sweatshops of Connecticut and Massachusetts, the soldiers of the Confederacy swung through the bleak New England countryside – aristocrats from the great plantations, farmer-boys from Georgia, mountaineers with rifles their forbears had carried at King's Mountain or Cowpens, Creoles from the Delta country, drawling Texans – all drawn together in freedom's cause. It was not that the descendants of the heroes of Lexington and Bunker Hill fought with less valor than their forebears; more likely it was the fundamental weakness of the principles for which the North strove which permitted the grey tide to roll irresistibly to the sea. How hollow now seem the perfervid appeals of Edward Everett calling upon New Englanders to emulate the example of the Revolutionary patriots of 1776. Exactly one year after Gettysburg, Boston fell to General John B. Gordon of Georgia – a good soldier, but a little careless with fire – his name now the very incarnation of devilry in the minds of the Daughters of the Grand Army of the Republic. On July 4th, 1864, Bob Toombs, true to promise, called the roll of his slaves on the steps of Fanieul Hall. To President Davis, Longstreet dispatched the famous telegram: "I beg to present you as a Fourth of July gift, the City of Boston, with 25,000 cans of baked beans, 150 tons of cod and Harvard College." Democracy in North America was safe. The War between the States was practically over.

It is true that the Mid-West remained unconquered. Many factors militated against an invasion of those backward states. The dreary and endless plains wore a forbidding aspect to soldiers from a section on which God had lavished warmth and greenness. Nor were the mulish tendencies of the Westerners with their grating accent encouraging to any idea of subjection. But more important, the South had no quarrel with the West. A unity of interest actually existed. The Abolitionists had skillfully driven the opprobrious epithet of "Slavery" as a wedge between the South and the West. Westerners who had served with Grant had seen for themselves, however, that slavery was essentially a form of master-servant relation that at worst was far more beneficent than the grinding labor system which the East had perverted to an attempt to destroy a peace-loving section of the Union. In a cabinet meeting President Davis, pointing significantly to New Orleans, counselled that the Western States be let well enough alone, sagaciously observing that the mandates of geography would eventually bring them into the Confederacy. His words proved prophetic. The brief and unhappy career of the Northwest Republic under the dictatorship of General William T. Sherman, with the South consistently refusing to yield a corridor to the sea, was terminated by a plea for admission into the Confederacy during the administration of

President Longstreet. Thus were answered the critics of Southern Independence to whom the idea of more than one nation seemed so repugnant. Manifest Destiny demanded a single sovereignty between the Atlantic and Pacific and such there was to be – the Confederate States of America. Today there are no more loyal members of the Confederacy than the Western states. Southerners are proud of the many Lee and Jeff Davis counties in that section. Only once has disaffection occurred in the Confederacy. During President Henry W. Grady's second term in office, Texas attempted to secede from the Confederate States after being thwarted in her attempt to annex South America. The revolt was stamped out. Since that time rebellion has not raised its ugly head in our land. "The Confederal Union – one and inseparable, it must be preserved."

But let us return for a moment to the problems that faced the South's statesmen in 1865. As the Union had been dissolved, the Eastern States were conquered territory. The urgency of re-establishing democracy among a people who had wandered so far from the teachings of Jefferson made it plain that thorough and immediate reconstruction of the North was an indispensable necessity. With their sordid pattern of living, symbolized by the flesh-pot and the slum, Northerners must be re-educated to the principles of the Republic when it was young. The de-Unionization of the North achieved to a considerable degree this needed revolution. To the long-suffering white laborer of that section Gettysburg afforded a welcome redistribution of economic opportunity. The Northern freedman has always been the object of Confederate solicitude, particularly around election time. The slogan "Forty spindles and a loom" became a famous one. Ironically enough, some Northerners refer to this constructive epoch as the "Tragic Era". Many of them never cease refighting the War Between the States.

But pressing business necessarily preceded any attempt at reconstruction. What of the criminal responsibility of the evil men who had led the Union into an aggressive war against states which had only sought to exercise the constitutional right of sucession? Were crimes against the law of nations – against humanity itself –

to go unpunished because of their very enormity or merely because the common law offered no precedent? Had not President Lincoln deliberately provoked the assault on Fort Sumter? What of war-mongers like Chase, Sumner, Seward and that breed who had contended that there was a higher law than the Constitution itself – who had taught the North that it had an "irrepressible conflict" with the South? What of Abolitionists like Garrison, Phillips, Everett and that ilk who had mouthed their right to destroy the South's hard-earned private property? What of arch-propagandists like Harriet Beecher Stowe with their creed of sectional hatred? Were these villipenders of the South to be permitted to live with impunity in villas purchased with the royalties of their libels? Were the acts of military criminals like "Beast" Butler to go unexpiated because they were committed under color of war? Surely those responsible for the loathsome Northern prisons should answer for the inhuman treatment given Confederate soldiers!

In the character of men such as Davis, Benjamin and Yancey there was something of vindictiveness. Over the protests of moderates like Stephens and Hill a Special Tribunal was created to try the war criminals. Indictments were brought against most of the "Yankee Gang". However, with the election of General Lee to the presidency of the Confederate States calmer counsels and a larger degree of tolerance prevailed. The prosecution was dropped. Lee's magnanimity met general approval in the South, where it was intuitively felt that it was not practical to draw any hard and fast line of demarcation between bad and good Yankees.

The rapid decline of the North during the 'Sixties and 'Seventies witnessed a corresponding growth in the South. Freed from its unholy matrimony with the North and from the tariff, the South entered a flourishing era. With the Confederacy's emphasis on States Rights, business has not been throttled by centralization of government and bureaucracy. In the Confederate States a bureau still means an article of bedroom furniture. The "Forty-Hour Week" means that an employee must work a minimum of forty hours, not a maximum. This industrial revolution in the South saw sleepy Southern towns mushroom into cities. When we see the huge metropolis of Atlanta with its population of three millions we marvel that it was ever the village of Marthasville. What a far cry is the great, bustling port of Savannah, with its million inhabitants and its harbor teeming with the world's shipping, from the "red river with a tranquil little fleet of merchantmen" that Thackeray saw in 1856. Savannah is, of course, the eastern terminus of the trans-continental Central of Georgia Railroad which runs to Los Angeles. Detroit takes pride in boasting that it is the "Atlanta of the West" as do Pennsylvanians in Pittsburg's claim to be the "Birmingham of the East." Southerners smile tolerantly when West Point is called the "V.M.I. of the North."

After the War the South had turned more and more to industry and away from the raising of cotton and magnolias and the production of juleps. Singular impetus in that direction occurred in the early 'Seventies. How were the wayward Northern States to pay the enormous reparations which simple justice to the South demanded? This dilemma was solved by the well-known Relief Act of 1871. Under it the North was relieved of all heavy industries adapted to aggressive war. The fairness which motivated the Confederate Congress in the Relief Act is nowhere better evidenced than by the fact that the Act required that slaves be tendered to the factory owners as payment for condemned property. In the celebrated "Legal Tender Cases" Chief Justice Bleckley of the Supreme Court upheld the validity of this progressive legislation. With the resulting emancipation of Northern labor the Northern States were eligible to be admitted into the Confederate States of America. Today only Maine and Vermont are still not sufficiently reconstructed to be taken in. However, they possess full colonial status.

In a world of iron and steam slavery was undoubtedly an anachronism. Once free from the harangues of the Abolitionists, Southerners were able to concede that fact. Many of the South's Negroes had already been sent North, where in a few years the freedom-loving Yankees had segregated them in the foul tenements of Harlem. If the North had believed in freedom for the slave, it seems that with even greater enthusiasm it espoused the cause of freedom from the ex-slave. By 1875 the last slave in the South had been set free. Today that institution exists only in California where some Northern-born residents keep Negro domestics in bondage.

Today the North is still in many ways the number one problem of the Confederate States. The Southern weekly magazines and press constantly subject the people of that section to ridicule and scorn, unable to comprehend the race riots, gangsterism, municipal corruption, bad manners and Communism prevalent in that region. Candid Northerners of the present generation are the first to admit the validity of much of this criticism. Less clear-seeing Yankees maintain that these North-baiting Southern editors are but carping critics. They complain that the Confederate Congress is unfair in refusing Northern dairy interests the right to color milk to resemble the South's famous Coca-Cola. It is true also that some of them disagree with the anti-North legislation the South sponsors every four years in the Confederate Congress. These measures include the FEPC Bill, which of course means "Fairly Evident Politics Concerned" Act. They also include the Civil Rights Bill which represents an attempt on the part of the South to secure constitutional rights for the native-born white population in the North which constitutes a hopeless minority compared to the predominant elements there. It is hoped in the South that enactment of the Civil Rights Bill will obtain for this hapless minority some measure of political freedom.

Yet there is a feeling in the South that the North, bad as it undoubtedly is, is not wholly beyond redemption. If the people of that section will only go back to work and raise their per-capita income to the confederal average much benefit will undoubtedly result to the American economy. Competent observers see that day coming. It is nothing less than the just desert of a people whom most Southerners are willing to admit have come a long way up from ruin and ignorance.

Leavening influences are undoubtedly at work in the New North. New York's governor is an up-and-coming young man who no longer lives in that section's musty past. Railroad rate discrimination against the North is the political stock-in-trade of this able Whig statesman who frankly tells his constituents that it is time to rejoin the Confederacy. This new political refrain is in some ways a relief from the cacophony of the conventional Northern demagogue whose *leitmotif* is the "damn-confederates." New York recently instituted condemnation proceedings against an exclusive club of Peachtree millionaires who for many years have maintained their summer residence on Long Island. This burgeoning spirit has spread to the Mid-West. Ohio is now even suggesting a candidate for the presidency. Gettysburg is still too close to our day for a New Yorker or an Ohioan to hope for national political success. But it is an encouraging sign for sectional good-will that such a suggestion can be seriously made.

What of the Confederacy in world affairs? It's foreign policy, dominated by matchless statesmanship of leaders cast in the mold of the Old South, has been a conspicuous success. A confederation which had its birth in the blood-bath of aggression has ever been watchful of tyranny, whether found in Massachusetts or in Moscow. A generation ago the Confederate States of America helped subdue Prussia's threat to world security. As a result of the Confederacy's participation in the League of Nations that organization has been a great force for world peace. Its decisive action when Germany tried to enter the Rhur Valley ended Hitler's brief career on the gallows. Having been forced to fight one war to make America safe for democracy, in the course of which the South played host to the Visigoths of Wisconsin and Indiana, and other wars to make the world safe, the Confederate States has never been disposed to tolerate conditions tending in any way toward yet another such conflict.

Today finds the nations of the world in contentment and peace. Richmond has well been called the "Earth's Capital." Some pessimists profess to see clouds on the horizon. "What of Russia?" they anxiously say. But ask a Southerner about the Russians and he is apt to smile and remind you that Josef Stalin himself was a South Georgia boy. And don't forget that the man who wields awesome power as the leader of the most powerful country in the Far East received his college degree at Athens, Georgia, where he majored in Confederate history.

Small wonder that February 8th is celebrated as a great confederal holiday in our country, a day on which the post-offices and banks are closed from Tybee Light to Puget Sound. We have much to be thankful for in this bright and happy land. But most of all we should be grateful for the fact that a fellow named Longstreet who was born on that day came up on time one hot July morning long, long ago.

My Life With Flora

(Garden Club of America banquet, Savannah, March 25, 1955. Reproduced here with minor revisions, including deletions and additions from two subsequent versions.)

I am flattered by the opportunity to speak before so lovely and distinguished a gathering of my fellow garden lovers of the Southern Zone. I should, however, warn our visitors, here and now, that no one from Savànnah who knows me has the slightest expectation that the degree of anticipation which my introduction has created will see realization.

The chairman of your Speakers' Committee was not very helpful in my selection of a subject. She told me that almost any old talk would do – as long as I didn't mention flowers. Apparently the very thought of gardens is abhorrent to the Garden Club of America. However, she did give me some ideas as to the general type of talk I should make. It is to be neither too long nor too short; philosophical and instructive without being dull or scholarly; and above everything else I must be extremely entertaining.

Now, before I say another word, let me warn this audience that I am no light after-dinner speaker. If anybody wants a heavy diet of post-prandial nourishment, call on me. I may look funny, but it ends right there. So take a good look at me right now and if that's what you are going to laugh at please get it out of your system. Not by nature, choice or inclination am I humorous. I never laugh. In fact, my wife says that the nearest thing she ever saw to a smile on my face is an expression of chagrin. My idea of a night's light reading is Burton's *Anatomy of Melancholy*. Boris Karloff is my favorite comedian and Lucretia Borgia has always been my conception of a woman with a sense of humor.

In my garden I grow no Sun Flowers or Sweet William, Baby's Breath or Smilax. I grow cancer root, mandrake, hemlock, various flesh-eating vines, toxicodendron and "maiden's ruin." That's the kind of after-dinner speaker who is supposed to amuse you tonight.

I mediated a long time about a subject. It is with regret that I announce my decision to speak in serious vein upon a subject which happens to be the very one I was warned to stay clear of – gardening. The title of my lecture tonight is: "The Dilemma of the American Garden Lover; the Problem, the Challenge – and the Lack of Any Solution."

It was some years ago that I took up gardening. I was over-golfed. I was coming home from the golf club cross, irritable and unrelaxed. I either had to give up the game or find some compensating relaxation. My doctor told me: "Golf is going to kill you, if you keep on. Get a real hobby. Anything to get your mind off your niblick. Get yourself a steed and a lance and take up jousting. Buy a harquebus or a falcon and go grousing." It was clear that my doctor was just as bad off mentally as I was. It was also clear that he needed some other diversion than Sir Walter Scott. But I took his advice. I decided to grow a garden.

First I read a lot of books on the subject. Then I made up my garden plan. It included a herbaceous border, a box hedge, a primrose path, and a vista. Neighbors will be far more impressed if you add a tennis court and a swimming pool. You cannot have a garden without a plan. But mine turned out to be what the neighbors mistook as a plot. How well I remember that first evening when I went out into the yard with my spade and began to dig in the soil. What excitement! (Not mine, the neighbors'.) It so happened that at the time the lady with whom I live in holy deadlock had gone out of town to visit a friend. Neighbors can be suspicious people. I thought I saw one of them peeping at me through her rear window. She was. She spread the word that I had cut Mrs. Lawrence into little pieces and was burying her in the garden. The talk didn't cease until my wife got back. Actually with fertilizer as cheap as it was at the time it was needless to consider anything as drastic as that. However, the price of ammonium phosphate and sulfate of potash has gone sky high since then!

I work awfully hard in my garden. My wife says very wittily that all I grow in my garden are ugly callouses. Oh, the thrill of having a spade in my hand! (It's even greater when you've got five spades!) Sometimes I get so weary relaxing in my garden I am barely able to make my way back from my two rose bushes outside to my Four Roses inside. When gardening tires you too much I suggest that you get a gardener. If possible, get Ava Gardner.

I once heard Judge Henry Hammond make a talk about relaxing with camellias. Here is what he said about lawyers and flowers:

"We lawyers must all get acquainted with the camellia. Lots of times my very heart and spirit are torn asunder. When I have lost a case, I am in a state of violent antagonism, and I make up my mind then and there to impeach the judge, or shoot him, and I feel that I would like to cut the throats of the jury with a dull knife. Then, when I go out to my garden, this camellia looks up and says, 'Don't take it so hard.' The camelia beckons me over and says, 'Come here; you have got us, and we love you. Forget about that stupid judge and that crazy half-baked jury. Come over here; we will temper this blow'. In a little while I am happy, and I have forgotten all the wrongs and outrageous injuries that have been done me." So Judge Hammond says.

Now, my camellias have never said one word to me. Something must be wrong with me. I have said a lot of things about camellias but they never reply.

But whether or not your flowers talk to you, I agree gardens can be very relaxing work. In fact, I have experimented scientifically with the various degrees of relaxation obtained by a garden. A good rum punch (preferably a Planter's Punch) is as good a way as any of finding out the amount of pleasure it gives you. Incidentally, I dealt with this feature of gardening in a talk I made before the Tulip & Julep club some years ago. Here is how you can determine the volume of your garden relaxation. Go out among your flowers without a Planter's Punch and note the amount of enjoyment you get. Then take one with you and see how much added pleasure your garden gives you. If you get none at all substitute Artillery Punch. Then try a second and a third. If X is the total of the initial pleasure experieñced in the garden, add the degree of relaxation you experience with the first drink and the second and the third. If the progression of your relaxation is arithmetical, that is X plus 1/2, plus 1, plus 1 1/2, then all very good. But if the relaxation progression is geometric, that is, 2 plus X with the first Punch; 4 plus X with the second and 8 plus X with the third or if you can't remember what the hell it is, then I suggest that you are the planter type rather than the gardener type.

One of the common mistakes that beginners in flower growing make is in not talking to a lawyer before starting out. Let me give you one illustration. Suppose your neighbor has a tree growing near the property line and its branches extend over on your side. What can you do about it? Well, under the common law you can lop off the overhanging branches right up to your property line. But you can't go any further. If you cut the branch beyond that line you are committing a trespass.

So, too, if the roots of your neighbor's tree extend over into your yard and draw moisture and food constituents required for your flowers you have the right to cut the trespassing roots off. You can cut them off right up to the property line. One must watch roots very carefully. If you allow the neighbor's roots to grow for a number of years over on your side of the property line you will be guilty of what the law calls laches – in other words, you have slept on your rights too long to get relief in court. You have got to watch those roots and intercept them as soon as they reach your property line. This is the kind of down-to-earth advice a lawyer can give you about your garden.

A few words about soil are improbably in order. Soil can be important to gardening. You have got to have soil unless you are growing a marine garden. And from what I have seen of you the last two days you are not very interested in water. Now soil is called *terra firma*. It consists of topsoil and bottom soil. If you do not have any bottom soil, sub-soil will do just as well. In fact, its name comes from being a substitute soil or sub-soil. Now, the best soil is loam. The ideal soil has been defined as rich, unctuous loam. This, however, is seldom found except in gardens of rich, unctuous people. But don't be discouraged. A real garden lover (and you must love your garden whether you like it or not) can overcome the handicap of poor soil. One only has to have a sense of humus.

The soil in my own yard was very poor. However, a green thumb can do a lot. I fortified and improved my soil by throwing into the yard all of my wife's old school annuals. I also threw into it all of her last year's books on the Goren system. I dumped into it all of the discarded candy into which my children had put their forefingers to make sure they were caramels. It is now my mint bed. Beer cans are excellent for improving soil. Get enough of them and you can have a beer garden.

I am trying not to use scientific terms before this audience. I am disappointed to see so few notebooks in the audience. Maybe you know all there is. But I always say (rather cleverly I think) that a good gardener is always a beginner. Somehow women *do* make the best gardeners. Eve made such a mess in the Garden of Eden they have been trying to make up for it ever since.

I was born with a peculiar affliction. My mother told me it was a curse laid on the family by an Irish ancestor (on my father's side, of course) who came over on the Mayflower with William the Conqueror. I hesitate to shock you. But here it is. [Show hand with bright green glove] People laughed at my deformity. But my mother consoled me. "It is not your Irish hand," she said, "it is your Iris hand." When I took up gardening I came to understand its true significance. Let me show you what I mean. Here is a plant which a few of you will recognize as the Drooping Diphtherium. Poor thing, it has hereditary lumbago – curvature of the stem. All this species needs is a green hand. [Magician's flower straightens upright]. You thought I didn't know about flowers, didn't you? No wonder that out in California people speak of Luther Burbank as "the Lawrence of the West."

Of fertilizer and plant nourishment I fain would speak next. You have heard of miracle drugs. Well, here is a miracle plant food I have developed. I call it 007. It has a secret agent in it. Take this little flower. Pitiful, isn't it? It is the *hysteria reticens*, a species of the shrinking violet. In fact, it is so bashful that it refuses to bloom in public. But a good plant food can work wonders with bashful blooms. Let's try 007 on the little fellow and see whether we can get a bloom. We will put some on and watch. [Magician's flower]. Upsy Daisy! Oh, my, the bloom's gone again. But that is all right. All you have to do is keep up the treatment.

People frequently pester me with questions as to what to do about pests, particularly borers. My advise to you is, "Don't invite them back." But the worst garden pest we have on the Georgia coast is the bittern. I have seen many a good garden go to seed because of the Bittern. I am speaking of the Angostura Bittern.

I have found that the best insecticide is the toad frog. I contend that no garden is complete without a toad. They thrive on insects. "Toady up to the toad," I always say. They are useful in another way. Sometimes we find parasitic growths in our garden such as mushrooms and toadstools. The toad is indispensable in determining whether you should eat them or not. Watch your toad. If he just sits there on the stool, it is not a mushroom. It is a "toadstool."

People tell me constantly that I should put more sex in my writings. So I will deal with that subject briefly. Flowers can be very useful in teaching your children the facts of life. Those pretty little devils lead quite a sex life. I learned all about it during my researches in cross-pollination. Why anybody should be cross about it, I don't know.

There comes a time when your children ask questions like "What does pollen do." "What is daddy good for?" This is the moment for you to tell them. Just as girls when sprinkled with perfume and decked in colorful frocks attract young men to them, so too nature dresses up her flowers, giving them beautiful aromas, in order to make them attractive to insects and birds.

But don't stop there. Give your daughter, Petunia, and your teen-age son, Pimpernel, the whole truth. (They probably know it anyhow.) Gather them around you some night and say it with flowers. Explain to them, and I borrow from an expert English gardener, how the pollen-grains from the "anthers on the pistil of one florescence are translated by the insect to the business end of the stigma of the other florescence and thence send out long thin rootlets down the central cavity of the style which enters the matured ovules and later create the seed-lobes or cotyledons" from which baby flowers grow.

If you put it to your daughter like that, you will likely keep her from ever going steady or going out at all. And maybe Pimpernel himself will stop running after that Kudzu girl down the street who grew up so fast.

This lecture would be entirely inadequate if I did not refer again to camellias. I have made a particular study of camellia grafts. I am never quite so happy as I am when I have a pair of shears in my hands. My wife says that I am a shear genius. I might say that I was somewhat put out when the lady who introduced me did not say anything about my writings on horticulture. She mentioned only my work in history. I will have you know that recently I had an article published in the *American Fungus Lovers' Year Book* entitled, "Grafting: How to Do it; Together with Helpful Hints on Getting Away With It."

I delivered a paper two years ago, at the Southern Zone meeting of the Affiliated Ragweed Clubs of America, entitled "Profit in Growing Weeds, or Marijuana Culture in the Low South." Incidentally, that is a good way to rid your garden of weeds. The Drug Enforcement officers will deweed it for you without charge.

The most revolutionary thing I have introduced in my work in grafting is to dispense with the scion. The scion, as you know, is the small branch of the camellia variety which you wish to reproduce and which you graft on to the understock. Now I don't like scions. I have yet to see one that amounted to anything. All of the scions I ever knew have been black sheep.

Tonight I am going to exhibit for the first time to an audience my masterpiece of camellia propagation, an entirely new species of camellia. But first let me go back a bit. A few years ago I took a trip through Upper Tibet. (There is no Lower Tibet.) One day as I wandered lonely in the Himalayas, all at once I saw a cloud, a host of rainbow flowers of such rare beauty as never had I beheld. I recognized the plant immediately. It was the lost *Otosclerosis*. I experienced the same thrill John Bartram felt near the Altamaha River when he first set eyes upon the lost *Gordonia*. My dear friend the Grand Lama insisted that they were plain old japonicas. They were camillias, as anyone as knowledgeable as I could see. I brought some shoots back home. I realized that I stood at the threshhold of a new era in camelliadom. Here was a plant so hardy it could withstand the hardest freeze. If I succeeded, we would no longer have to call off the Savannah Camellia Show every year.

My problem was to graft a shoot of the Tibetan flower in such a manner that it could withstand our summer climate. After considerable study I selected the ligustrum as my understock. The graft took. A seedling resulted. Then a miracle took place.

Observe my masterpiece! See the rainbow-colored blooms and the bright colors of the petals. Admire the texture of the stamen. Note the symmetry. But this plant has another unusual quality. People say that there can be no perfect flower without fragrance. Well, this blooming camellia is the only one on the earth that smells. And does it smell!

Recently I tried to enter my masterpiece in the Norfolk Camellia Show. They turned me down. They called me a quack and said my plant should be called the "Grandiflora Humbugosa." All over the garden walls in Virginia people scribbled "Go home, Lawrence."

And it is high time that I do that. But before I conclude this lecture, you will agree that my *chef d'oeuvre* of camellia culture deserves official recognition by your club. The only honor I have ever received before was from the Amaryllis, Texas, Chapter of the League for the Preservation of Endangered Bugs. It was on the occasion when I delivered my classic paper entitled "The Care and Feeding of Aphids."

Too long has my work and my many contributions to horticulture been ignored. Tonight I am going to make sure. I have arranged personally for your honoring me.

I now pin upon my chest this medallion and ribbon. On it is inscribed, "In honor and appreciation from the Garden Clubs of America of one who has done so much to improve the art of flower culture and more especially for his revolutionary development of the species of camellia known as the "Grand Lama."

My fellow gardeners of the Southern Zone, may I respond briefly. I deeply appreciate this honor. I am greatly moved by this token of your appreciation. The honor you have given me is even greater than the honorarium. I am so moved that I can't go on further. So I bid good night to you. May all your dreams be *sub rosa*!

Madeira and Moonshine

(Annual banquet of the Madeira Club, a group which gathers periodically for an evening of literary and gastronomical pursuits, Savannah, 1979. Editor's Note: While Madeira is world-famous for its fine wines, the vicinity of Metter, Georgia, is locally famous for its illicit liquor.)

Malmsey is great; Sercial is better
But give me the vintage brewed around Metter.
Distilled in the pinewood; aged in troughs,
Bottled in jars and stashed in hay lofts,
Oh what bouquet! One swig and a smell,
And a drinker has quaffed the water of hell.
The nectar of the gods came from the vine
But what can compare with Georgia moonshine?

Part II

Legally But Not Legalistically Speaking

Bird-Watching in the Bankruptcy Court

(Excerpt from remarks at ceremony at which Hon. Herman Coolidge took the oath as Bankruptcy Judge, Savannah, July 1, 1975.)

There is one aspect of Mr. Coolidge's accomplishments with which I was frankly not familiar until yesterday. I learned that he is one of the outstanding ornithologists in this part of the country, a former president of the Georgia Ornithological Society, and one of the most indefatigable of bird watchers.

Indeed, his interest in our feathered friends is such that I have been somewhat concerned lest, in the course of his new career, he will miss them so much that he will want to return to bird-watching. However, I have good news for him. Judge Bowen tells me that many strange birds come to roost in the Bankruptcy Court, including species unknown even to an expert like Mr. Coolidge.

There is the debtor species which includes the largebilled kite, the unsecured loon and the involuntary cuckoo. He will also find the night owl and double-breasted swallowtail, a bird that is frequently seen in the company of the red-headed vampire.

Among the birds of passage that have no homesteads Herman will see the asset-hiding sap-sucker and the vanishing species called the migratory road-runner. Another migrant is the conglomerate skimmer. A feathered friend frequently seen in the bankruptcy court nests on the bars along our coast. I refer to the angostura bittern.

Then, there are the birds of prey such as the falcons and the hawks, which, season after season, unsuccessfully pursue the National League bunting. Then there is the common creditor bird, which debtors classify as a member of the vulture family.

Finally, he will see the oceanic birds that fly high and wide such as Mother Carey's Chicken, Incorporated, now under Chapter X of the Bankruptcy Act.

And so this Court is very pleased to be able to inform Mr. Coolidge that as bankruptcy judge he will be able to continue his pastime of watching his feathered friends.

How to Reduce Appellate Case Loads

(Report to district and circuit judges of the Fifth Circuit at Judicial Conference, Houston, Texas, 1976.)

Chief Judge Brown's State of the Judiciary message to the Judicial Conference presents a lamentable and lugubrious picture of the present caseload situation and the future outlook. His presentation of the troubles of our overworked circuit court is replete with workload projections and tables showing what lies ahead. The Chief has given us an alarming forecast as to what can be expected in the disposition of non-preference appeals which, of course, includes all diversity cases. Of the 514 new non-preference cases filed in fiscal year 1977, nonc will be heard in 1977; only 30% in 1978, 52% in 1979. The next 18% will be reached in 1980. Of the new non-preference cases filed in 1979, none will be heard in 1980, none in 1981, none in 1982, and only 148, or 25.6% in 1983, with the balance of the 430 cases being heard between 1984 and 1987 – a delay of six to nine years from the date of docketing to the argument.

Judge Brown has requested me to report on what actions were taken at the meeting of the District Judges earlier this week.

There is little to report. The session was takcn up almost wholly with a wrangle among the judges over a resolution which proposed that our association present a petition to Congress for redress of grievances under the First Amendment over the failure to increase the compensation of federal judges. In the end, after an acrimonious debate, the proposed resolution was tabled and all the distributed copies were gathered up from the district judges and destroyed. Under a motion to table, all references in the minutes concerning this subject were ordered to be deleted.

So I have nothing to report. I am under the gag rule. However, in reporting on the District Judges meeting this week I can deal with the Association's reaction to your State of the Judiciary message and the unfortunate tribulations of the Court of Appeals for the Fifth Circuit. We deeply sympathize with the problems and woes caused by increase of appeals from the district courts. After much study, we trial judges offer a plan which we believe will reduce your appellate caseload to an irreducible minimum within a few years, provided your court will follow our recommendations.

The district judges' solution for excessive appeals is a simple one. We call the concept "Toleration of Error Below," or for short, TEB or "teb." The fundamental concept and theory behind "teb" is that the greater the volume of reversals and remands by a circuit court of appeals the greater will be the volume of appeals the following year. The converse is that the larger the percentage of affirmances, the lower the volume of appeals. It's that simple – just as easy as falling off a backlog.

Statistical studies by the district judges in our Fifth Circuit reveal a high rate of reversal and remand. We call the ratio the Annual Reversal-Remand Percentage, or ARRP or "arp," for brevity. It is arrived at by dividing the number of reversals and remands into the number of appeals during the year. In determining the "arp" percentage, we eliminate all cases placed on the summary calendar. We do so on the theory that the "Arp" formula should not accord weight to appeals the appellate court has not weighed. I am not criticizing the no-argument rule.

However, I call attention to the fact that a century ago Chief Justice Bleckley observed in one of his decisions that a lawyer should not be cut off from making an argument when his "address is warm in his bosom, alive and undelivered . . . for it is not impossible that a suppressed speech may occasion more mental torture than a lost cause."

The raw reversal percentage is subject to a further adjustment. Appellate judges live by correcting the errors of others through adhering to their own. Trial judges recognize that the Law of Self-Preservation is applicable to the appellate courts. Only reversals justify the existence of an appellate court. Accordingly, we make due allowance in the Arp formula for a minimum number of reversals and remands.

Such is the concept of "Toleration of Error Below." It is somewhat revolutionary. But the crisis of the Fifth Circuit demands bold and imaginative measures. We must preserve our appellate resources and energy.

The Fifth Circuit can turn the trend of ever-increasing appeals completely around. If you will only reduce your reversal rate by a small percent the results will be astounding. Our statistical studies indicate that appeals decrease at least 5% for each 1% decrease in the court's annual reversal-remand percentage. Taking cases up to the higher court will soon lose all appeal. It is a striking illustration of Lawrence's Law of Diminishing Appeals.

Judge Brown, you are going to have to lower your "Arp."

A Federal Judge's Prayer

(Excerpt from address to Atlanta Bar Association, Atlanta, March 17, 1971.)

In the past two and a half years, despite lack of training, experience, competence or inclination, I have found myself telling officials how to run schools, including the hiring and firing and promotion of teachers and principals; how to run the Georgia State Prison and local jails; instructing local draft boards who should be inducted and the armed forces who should be discharged after induction; running restaurants; deciding how long high school students can wear their hair or when the fuzz above a teenage boy's lip becomes a mustache; operating beauty salons; telling movie operators, bookstores and newspapers what is pornographic and obscene; instructing aldermen what package shops to license or de-license; adjudicating who can play in a golf tournament on a municipal course; telling jury commissioners who must be on the jury lists; serving as employment manager for firms and corporations, and so on.

Sometimes when I go to bed at night I feel like saying a prayer and it would go something like this:

> *Dear Lord, on bended knee I pray you, tomorrow send me a plain old tort case. Or if You can't do that, a suit on a simple contract in writing will do just as well. That's a little enough favor to ask even if I have gotten rusty on the common law since I've been on this Court.*

And deliver me, oh Lord, from any 2254s or 1981s, 1983s, 1985s or any 2000s (a-e, inclusive). You got troubles, I know, in enforcing Chapter 20, subsections 3–17, inclusive, of the Book of Exodus. But it can't be much worse than what we federal judges have under Title 42. And if You care about me, Lord, don't send me any class actions, whatever they are.

It's not that I mind work. You know me better than that, Lord. It's just that I'm not a pedagogist, penologist, theologist, sociologist, cosmetologist, tonsorialist, restaurateur, literary censor or personnel director.

And another thing, please don't put me on any more three-judge courts. Lord knows, I got enough trouble agreeing with myself – much less trying to convince two other durn fools.

Now, I know You don't have much contact with the United States judges in the Northern District of Georgia. You can't be everywhere. We realize that. But for Your information, Chief Judge Smith's got six district judges besides himself up in that District. And down here in the Southern District I got nobody but me. I'm a Chief with no Indians and it looks like everybody's on the warpath against me.

So please send me some judicial help. I've been without it for two long years. I don't care how little law the additional judge knows. That doesn't matter. He can learn the job as he goes along. The main thing he's going to need is a camper and an appetite for catfish stew and squirrel mull because he's going to spend a lot of his time out in rural Georgia.

Now, Lord, I'm not trying to run Your business. But some day You've got to put an end to the invidious discrimination against me and give me the equal protection of the Ten Commandments and all the recent amendments thereto.

And one more thing, Lord. Watch Your step. I've got news for You. You've got real competition down in this section. The first thing You know the Fifth Circuit Court of Appeals is going to permanently enjoin You from this discrimination against me. Of course, I realize there's a question of service on You under the Long-Arm Statute. But let me warn You – that's not going to bother the Fifth Circuit very much.

AMEN

Ray Donald Katzensky vs. United States

IN THE UNITED STATES DISTRICT COURT FOR THE

SOUTHERN DISTRICT OF GEORGIA

SAVANNAH DIVISION

RAY DONALD KATZENSKY,

Plaintiff

VS. CIVIL ACTION NO. 3197

UNITED STATES OF AMERICA,

Defendant

ORDER

Petitioner who is a prisoner at the Georgia State Prison seeks to file in *forma pauperis* a petition for writ of habeas corpus. He alleges that he was convicted in 1970 in the Superior Court of DeKalb County of armed robbery and sentenced to a term of 20 years. He does not claim that his constitutional rights have been violated in any way but asks that the Court order his release so that he may join a group of Chilean "freedom fighters".

This Court is, of course, without power to modify state sentences or to release state prisoners.* The petition is dismissed and will be filed for record purposes only.

This October 12th, 1973.

ALEXANDER A. LAWRENCE, Chief Judge
United States District Court
Southern District of Georgia

**I am aware that in November, 1864, convicts were released from the Penitentiary at Milledgeville who volunteered to serve in the State militia in opposing Sherman's March to the Sea. However, the Governor of Georgia authorized the release, not the Confederate District Court. Besides, it was a better cause.*

Jones vs. Ault, 67 F.R.D. 124

George C. JONES, Petitioner,

v.

Dr. Allen L. AULT *et al.*, Director of the Georgia Board of Correction and Offender Rehabilitation and Members thereof, and Joe S. Hopper, Warden, Georgia State Prison, Reidsville, Georgia, Respondents (two cases).

NOS. CV474-279, CV474-293.

United States District Court,
S. D. Georgia,
Savannah Division.
Nov. 19, 1974.
Final Order Dec. 13, 1974.
67 F.R.D. 124

George C. Jones, *pro se.*

ORDER

LAWRENCE, Chief Judge.

Petitioner, an inmate at Georgia State Prison at Reidsville, seeks to file in *forma pauperis* a civil rights petition pursuant to 42 U.S.C. § § 1983, 1985. Jones alleges that he is the subject and victim of a "Behavior Mofification Program" conducted at the prison and that the "controlling system is a watchful eye of the State through electronic surveillance upon the human body . . . ." He asserts that the surveillance system "combs" his body and "wantonly monitors and picks up sounds and voices, but is also tuned directly to plaintiff's brain".

Petitioner says that the "machine apparatus used to perfect such felonious and fierce acts perhaps consist in part; EEG, EKG, transmitters and other electric gadgets. Also, from these machines and electric transmitting devices comes an electric current (voltage unknown) that penetrates the complete body of plaintiff causing ill effects, itch, a heated chest, a heated abdomen, an attack upon the brain and heart which is severe pain and harassment to Plaintiff."

Petitioner seeks injunctive relief and $500,000 in damages from the defendants.

Jones claims that he is a "guinea pig" and that the behavior modification system is a violation of his First, Fourth, Fifth, Eighth and Fourteenth Amendment rights. He maintains that the State has "no right without any permission from plaintiff to probe his mind and body with electric current or parabolic sound waves".

This Court is intrigued by the alleged "Behavior Modification Program" at Reidsville and the machine or device by which such is accomplished. It must be conceded that a mechanism which can probe the human mind, monitor thoughts and achieve behavioral control over a person is not without significance. If it actually exists, the brainscan machine would appear to represent a distinct advance over prior art in the field of extra-sensory perception.

I take it that petitioner is claiming that the prison authorities at Reidsville utilize a thought-control machine by which electronic or sonic waves are transmitted to his brain so as to produce behavioral modification. Quite possibly, the alleged device achieves control of one's behavior by concentrating electronic impulses on that part of the brain known as the "thalamus"–a cerebral area believed by some medicopsychologists to influence or affect "adjustment to the environment" when externally stimulated by a means or mechanism adapted to that purpose. See Walker Percy, *Love in the Ruins* (Farrar, Straus & Giroux, New York, 1971), p. 27.

It is claimed that the machine is also capable of reading minds. I gather that psychoretrieval is accomplished by electronic waves being transmitted to the inmate's cerebellum where they "listen" to the micro-thought impulses generated by the process of mentation. The machine then transmits such impulses to a parabolic reflector in the prison where the innermost thoughts of inmates are decoded by some process with which this Court lacks familiarity.[1] We must not be too precipitate in disbelieving and discrediting scientific miracles. It was, I believe, the celebrated Harvard astronomer, Simon Newcomb, who at the time the Wright Brothers were tinkering with their flying contraption, pontificated thusly:

> "The demonstration that no possible combination of known substances, known forms of machinery, and known forms of force can be united in a practical machine by which man shall fly long distances through the air, seems to the writer as complete as is possible for a demonstration of any physical fact to be."

The meliorative possibilities of such a device for the benefit of humanity are considerable if it stays in proper hands. However, petitioner thinks that it is in bad hands.[2] He alleges that his thoughts are read and his behavior controlled without his consent and in violation of his First Amendment right of free thinking and his Fourth Amendment guarantee against unreasonable search and seizure.[3] This Court perceives a distinction between mass thinking achieved by the media, on the one hand, and the surreptitious control of thinking, on the other hand, by the use of electronic apparatus.

It would seem that a machine that represents a major breakthrough in metaphysics would have been patented in the United States Patent Office. Apparently, it has not been.[4] This and other factors create reservations and doubts in the Court's mind as to granting relief to plaintiff at this stage.

In petitioner's answer to the questions propounded by the Court, he admits that he has not seen the machine nor has any other inmate, to his knowledge. "But we know that they exist by the powers of perfection." Jones says that cross-examination of "Behavioral Biologists" and psychiatrists is necessary in order to prove that he is being subjected to a Behavior Modification Program by use of "parabolic waves or a strange alien current or radiation waves". Plaintiff informs the Court that the device may be located at Reidsville but that the "most likely place" at which the electronic machines are set up is at the Central State Hospital at Milledgeville.

The waves particularly attack the pituitary gland which, petitioner says, is the most important portion of the "emotional brain".

However, they are directed at various other parts of his body, causing such symptoms as itch between the legs and his private parts and in the rectal area; hunger after eating; sleeplessness; sexual self-excitation; loss of memorary; sluggishness; depression; paranoia; fire in the stomach and chest; migraine, *et cetera.*

Plaintiff alludes to the development of sophisticated electronic devices which are capable of picking up whispers in a room and broadcasting them to a receiver a half block away. I am cognizant of modern developments in that field. Indeed, space-age, microminiaturized electronic gadgets make it possible to attach radio receivers to experimental animals with implanted electrodes being activated by remote control so that selected regions of the hypothalmus may be electrically stimulated to produce aggressive or submissive behavior as well as sexual and appetitive responses in animals.[5]

This experimentation in stimulating appropriate regions of the brain stem to produce behaviorial response in animals is notable. So are the modern advances in electroencephalography (EEG).[6] But compared with the Behavior Modification device at Reidsville the developments referred to represent the difference between a roman candle and Pioneer XI. The point is not the infinitesimally minute possibility that electropsychological science has developed to the stage of reading and controlling the human mind through electronic or sonic waves. The point here is that the claim of the existence of a machine capable of achieving such fantastic results is supported by the merest speculation, surmise or *ipse dixitism.*

Accordingly, the complaint brought in this jurisdiction is dismissed and will be filed for record purposes only. The action transferred to the Southern District is also dismissed.

NOTES

1. I am not unfamiliar with the general subject of remote control over the mind. It came to my notice a year ago when a petition was filed by an inmate of a federal prison who alleged that the Parole Board employed electronic sensory eavesdropping and brain recording equipment to produce in him a state of "moronism." See *Boyce v. United States Parole Board* (S.D., Ga., C.A. 3224, 11/16/75).

2. Such was the fate that befell the "lapsometer", a super-sophisticated stethoscope of the human spirit, capable of making readings in pinheaded areas of the brain and of fathoming, measuring and treating hidden anxieties, depressions, inner conflict and lusts. See Percy, *Love in the Ruins*, op. cit., *passim*.

3. The Fourth Amendment contention raises the questions of whether thought interception by means of electronic brain-scanning is a search or seizure of one's person and whether or not thoughts by themselves constitute "effects" within the meaning of such constitutional provision. Government eavesdropping by recording a person's oral statements represents a "search and seizure." *Katz vs. United States*, 398 U.S. 347, 88 S.Ct. 507, 19 L.Ed. 2d 576. Is the fact that one's thoughts, rather than spoken or written words, are intercepted significant? And what of the effect of the recognized right of prison authorities to subject inmates to intense surveillance and search without the necessity of obtaining warrants. See *People vs. Hernandez*, 229 Cal. App.2d 143, 40 Cal.Rptr. 100, 229 cert. den. 381 U.S. 953, 85 S.Ct. 1810, 14 L.Ed. 725. Perhaps, however, these speculations about the Fourth Amendment contention possess a degree of idleness at this stage.

4. This Court is not unaware that prison authorities utilizing thought control machines are unlikely to reveal the existence or operation of so revolutionary a device.

5. After this Court's first Order, an identical complaint filed by Jones in the Northern District of Georgia was transferred to this jurisdiction for convenience of parties and witnesses. That action is consolidated with the case now before this Court.

6. C.U.M. Smith, *The Brain, Towards an Understanding* (Putnam Sons, New York, 1970), 236–239, 244–245. "The implantation of electrodes in order to control [animal] behaviour has become a common technique . . . Among the specific behaviour patterns that have been evoked by electrical stimulation at different sites in the brain are eating, drinking and fighting." Keith Oatley, *Brain Mechanisms and Mind* (E. P. Dutton, New York, 1972), 127. The technical papers and studies cited by those two authors include: J.M.R. Delegado, "Free behaviour and brain stimulation", 6 *International Review of Neurobiology* (1964), 349–449.

A Defendant's Pre-Sentence Dreams

(Edward J. Sistrunk, a part-time minister who comes from the Edisto River south of Charleston, operates a real estate business in that city. He appeared before a jury in the federal district court at Savannah on a charge of violating the United States Code through a fraudulent scheme carried out by use of interstate telephone. The following exchange is from the official court record.)

THE COURT: Reverend, what would you like to say?

REVEREND SISTRUNK: I would like to say this, Judge. If it is possible, I don't know whether it could be done or not, it's up to you now because I'm in your hands, but I wrote you a letter and I want the Marshal to read it. Have you got it?

THE MARSHAL: Don't know anything about it. It might have gone to the office.

THE COURT: Did one come in?

THE MARSHAL: Not to my knowledge.

THE COURT: What did you say in it?

REV. SISTRUNK: Well, on last Sunday night the first week I spent in jail here, I had a dream. And, that dream indicated that I was on the Edisto River. They brought me to the river. And, there was three mens there, standing up looking in that river. And, when I got there close enough to them, one of them jumped off in that river. And, the two men standing there said to me, "You get that man." And I said to him that the water was too deep. And, then, the one that was standing in front looked at me and he said, "I AM THE LORD." When he said that, I just jumped in the river. And I didn't get no further than knee deep and I caught the man by his hand and I pulled him out. And, when we got out the water, it was a long sheet of white paper saying there was no $12,000 sales contract, be not guilty. The next night, that was Monday night, was the same thing. Tuesday night, it was the same thing, and I got up and started to the rail. There was a big guard standing there. And I watched him and he said, "What's wrong with you? You look like you're sick." And I said, "I had a dream. And, it's been on me now for three nights. And, I've been praying in jail. And, I've been preaching all my life and I asked the Lord, 'Why?' And, He showed me that. And I said, 'I want to get in to the Judge.' And He said, 'Reverend,' said, 'I would be glad to help you, but the only way you can get to that judge is through the Marshal.' He said, 'You ask the Marshal and ask him to make an appointment with the Judge to sit down and talk.'" And I kind of got satisfied, and I laid back down again.

The final dream was I went right straight back to that same river, that's the Edisto River, that's the place that I was born. Then I met one of the mens coming by with three sheets of paper in his hand, and he said to me "You go to the court house: I'm going to try you tomorrow." And when he turned and went to the left I discerned it was Your Honor. I said "This is Judge Alexander," and you just walked on. And when you were coming to me your robe was mist-like, like it was fog. But, when it turned to the left as you were going in that direction, it turned white. I said, "Who is this? Is this Judge. . ." He said "Yeah, this is me." Then, I turned around in this direction and looked back. And there was a black car behind me coming and two men got out of it and handcuffed me. The big fat one said, "We got to take you back to court." But when he put the handcuff on me, the handcuff turned into a snake, and that's why I was crying, and it bit him. And he went back to his car with his hands out, and the one on the other side said, "Well, you got him?" He said, "Yeah, we got him." Then he come around and said, "You got no handcuff on." Then he take off his handcuff and put it on me, and the handcuff break into pieces. And it went to the ground. And we look on at the car, and it was something like a snake, and that thing went out into that river and it multiplied itself into seven heads and ten horns. And one of the men said to me, said, "Reverend, let's go." One man said, "get in the car and let's go." And we drove, we come right to the table. And I come on in here and sit right there. You was standing in that door like you come in here. Leaning up against the door. And then the juries come down, and something like a rail on a railroad track, twelve of them sitting on that together. And two men was standing, I think. And that thing come right down this aisle and turn to the right. And stopped. And when it stopped they all got up and they take their seat. You came up, and when you got up on the stand, your robe turned white. It wasn't a black robe like it used to be. It turned white. And you sit down and you say, "Reverend," I hear you as plain as day, said, "I want you to take the stand and defend yourself." And when I got up to that rail that they come down on and put my foot up on it, there's a big hole, a *big* hole, and it dropped in there. And when it dropped in there, it was that same snake but there was thirteen numbers on him. And you hand me a sword and you say, "Cut your way to the witness stand." And I got that sword, and I started cutting. And I cut twelve length, and at the head of the length it was a man's head. And I back up from it. I said, "Judge, that's not a snake," I said, "that's a man in there." Then, the jury stood up and run around in this direction, and got behind the man and was saying, "You, you, you, you, you" just like that. And they stomped their foot, and pointed their finger at me. "You, you, you, you." And, at that time, I wake up. When I wake up, the guard was to the door. And I said "I would like to see Judge Alexander," I said, "because this is something unusual to me." And he said "Reverend, ain't nobody going to get in touch with him but go through the Marshal." And I sat down, and I wrote the Marshal a letter telling him that make arrangements with you that I wanted to talk with you. Because there's something about you that God showed me. That you are a clean man, as far as in your heart, with me. And He was good enough to show you to me in my vision. Hard as I've been praying, I prayed three nights and three days, didn't stop. See how I've fell off? Didn't eat anything because I've never been in this before. And I've been preaching for forty-two years and I asked the Lord "Why?" And He showed me that it was a contract, participating in this thing that I thought they had, but He said the $12,000 sales contract they don't have. Said I wasn't guilty. I thought that was the price of the house.

THE COURT: Who said that?

REV. SISTRUNK: The man's hand. You see, whenever I had the dream and I reached down and pulled the man up out of the water, instead of I pulling up a man, his hand turned to a white piece of paper. And on that white piece of paper it said, "There is no $12,000 sales contract."

THE COURT: A manifestation of God?

REV. SISTRUNK: That was the dream, a manifestation. Then I take it and hand it to the man who say he is the Lord. That's what confused me. He tell me to give it to the Judge, but I didn't thought you would be there. I didn't have the least idea that you would be in that kind of tranquility with the Spirit. And, you didn't make myself known to you.

THE COURT: I've been overruled by the Fifth Circuit Court of Appeals and by the Supreme Court of the United States, but God never has overruled me yet.

REV. SISTRUNK: No, I wasn't saying that. And, I said now, wonder why that this happened. The last portion of that dream, with this, you tell me don't shut that hole. See, I tried to put it back out. You said, "Left it open." And I said "I want to talk to you in private." But, it looked to me like I couldn't get to you, so I just thought I'd have to tell it to you when you get the letter.

THE COURT: You got to me today.

REV. SISTURNK: Right, and when you get the letter. . . .

THE COURT: You've already talked me out of two months.

REV. SISTRUNK: But, I'm saying I want you to know, I am not trying to evade the issue. I believe that there is something that I want to say to you and it is not going to take no effect. And I hope it doesn't, and I hope it do. I never had a contract, and I didn't know it until – and I meant to ask you this morning, and I'll be finished. I want you to explain it, if you got the contract I want you to read it. That's all. That's all I'm concerned about.

THE COURT: I can't do that.

REV. SISTRUNK: You can't?

THE COURT: The jury that said "You, you, you, you, you," they're the ones that did that. I can't do anything to say "Yes, yes, yes, yes." I will agree on one thing: the Reverend Mack, do you know him?

REV. SISTRUNK: Yes, he ordained me.

THE COURT: Do you know what he said about you?

REV. SISTRUNK: What is that?

THE COURT: He said if Reverend Sistrunk has done wrong we don't condone it, but we can't unfrock him; he will be a preacher right on, and a good one he is, too.

REV. SISTRUNK: Right, he ordained me in 1958. I'm the only preacher on the District that has a combination of jobs.

THE COURT: Well, let's get down to some mundane affairs, terrestrial rather than celestial.

* * * *

(The Reverend Edward J. Sistrunk was convicted by the jury. The Court gave him a two-year sentence which was probated to three months, followed by three years of supervised probation and the restitution of $320 to the party defrauded. Sistrunk promptly paid that sum, whereupon the Court reduced his sentence to one month in jail.)

From Rabun Gap to Tybee Light

(Georgia Bar Association luncheon, Clayton, Georgia, February 1950. Excerpt.)

"From the mountains" or "Rabun Gap",
Georgia politicians yap,
"To the sea" or "Tybee Light",
With their oratorical might.
Coming from the Georgia coast,
I should be the first to boast
Of Tybcc Light's effulgent gleam
(So, at any rate, 'twould seem.)
It's like I thought I ne'er would see,
Alas, Alack! 'Twas not to be!
Last night I saw what changed my mind
And now confess we're far behind.
For through the dark and stormy night
It's beacon shines not half so bright,
Compares, in fact, not one small bit
To a North Georgia jurist when he's lit.

ACKNOWLEDGEMENT

The lines from *John Brown's Body* (copyright 1927, 1928) by Stephen Vincent Benét (published by Holt, Rinehart & Winston, Inc.; copyright renewed 1955, 1956 by Rosemary Carr Benét) are used by permission of Brandt & Brandt Literary Agents, Inc.